The Angel Mystic's

Manifesting Manual

AN EASY GUIDE TO MANIFESTING

by Amanda Tooke
"The Angel Mystic"

First published in Great Britain by Amanda Tooke

Copyright © 2020 Amanda Tooke

ISBN: 978-1-913898-05-2
Also available as an Amazon best selling Ebook

Book & Cover Design by Russell Holden

Pixel Tweaks Publications
SELF PUBLISHING MADE SIMPLE

www.pixeltweakspublications.com

Acknowledgements

Thank you to all my clients who support and follow my work - this book is for you. I hope it changes your life like the process I share within it has changed mine.

I also want to mention my team of helpers from "The Upstairs" - without them this book would not have been written in such a short period of time. I started it 3 years prior to finishing it and kept putting it off. Once I knuckled down it was completed very quickly with their help.

Also, thanks to my daughter, Coralie, who kept nudging me to finish it, and the gentle requests from clients for the next book following on from - Do I have an Angel?

Thank you to everyone who shared their stories: Christina Butler, Simon Clarke, Jane Mate, Elizabeth Walton, Nancy Triplett, Kim Snow, Julie, Purvi and Angela.

I dedicate this book to my wonderful family,
who always support me.

They are my everything
and without them I am nothing.

The Author

Amanda Tooke " The Angel Mystic".

Spiritual Teacher
International Psychic
NLP Coach
Hypnotherapist
Practitioner of Time Line™ Therapy
Reiki Master & Natural Born Healer
Writer
Angel and Law of Attraction Specialist
Creator of The MAP – Manifesting Abundance Process
Who turns the "WooWoo" into "Woohoo" in your life!

Introduction

Welcome to this awesome adventure in which we shape and re-mould your life into one packed with abundance in all areas. I love the word abundance and it can really relate to whatever you want it to be. It can be money, it can be love, it can be health, it can be business success. It can be the really little stuff, the big stuff, the material stuff, and of course, the inner stuff. Whatever it is for you, you always use the same process to manifest it.

Before we even start on this adventure I need to tell you where I am writing this from.

This is my second book. My first book Do I have an Angel? was written squished in around my busy life. Most mornings I got up super early before the school run to get a couple of uninterrupted hours in before the crazy busy day started.

It was written like that because it had to be, I didn't have time, money or resources to do it any other way. I had two children to take care of, a business to run, clients to see and not a spare penny to do what I have done this time.

This time it is completely different. I am starting writing this book in the most idyllic pale pink beach house overlooking a bay in Anglesey, Wales. Just me and my little dog, Ellie, with glorious sunshine and beach walks to break up the writing.

I have taken a whole week to hide myself away and indulge myself in the most luxurious surroundings and amazing setting. Doing what I have always wanted to do, write with no distractions and get the frame work of this book in place.

The difference this time is that I have been following what I am about to teach you in this book.

I have followed it to the letter and have been doing it for quite some time, I have mastered the art of manifesting and am about to teach you to do the same.

My life been has transformed by doing what I share in this book and I am fortunate to be able to spend a considerable amount of money to treat myself to this experience. I have worked on my self-worth and stopped getting in my own way (we all do it). After all, this is an abundant Universe we are in and this book will give you simple, easy and fun guidance to how you can tap into the abundant flow and have what you really want too.

Let me tell you how this house came about, it was through the magic that is present all the time for all of us. My hope for you is that you tap into the magic too. So, I did a vision board over a weekend about 4 weeks before starting writing this book.

I collected lots of images and one of them was of this house. I had seen it the previous year and thought I would love to stay there. It was picture perfect and by the coast my dream location. I also felt compelled to stick on top of the house the words "Write Your Book". So I did exactly that, even though it looked quite strange it felt right. I was following my intuition and my guidance.

I went to bed that night and woke up the next morning with a huge intuitive nudge, knowing I had to check availability on this very cottage. Sure enough the only week available was my birthday week. I knew it was meant to be, it was waiting for me, I was sure of that. I booked it straight away without checking with the rest of the family about their plans. I was going, I had a book to write. So here it is, welcome to The Angel Mystic's Manifesting Manual.

I am going to teach you in this book how to decide what it is you want and how you can manifest it. As you will come to understand clarity is key. I will show you how you can feel abundant in all areas of your life and get inner peace too, as for me that is always the ultimate manifestation. Plus, of course I will help you to follow your guidance just like I did to write this book and do every day.

In this book I will give you all the tools you need to manifest and share some real life examples of mine and of clients I have worked with.

So before we start, let me tell you about my journey, so you know anything is possible.

I am Amanda Tooke, I am around half a century old when writing this book and I wish I had discovered my manifesting process much earlier in my life as it would have made things far easier than it has been. I am a bit quirky and love to laugh, I have done tons of personal development over the years and quite honestly I have got to a place that I can say I quite like myself. The laughing and liking yourself are really important in manifesting as you will see further on. Even better if you can love yourself, but honestly I am still working on that.

I grew up in Rainford with my parents, brother and Nana who lived with us. It was a lavish life for some years as my Dad was very successful in business. This is great in parts as we had many fabulous experiences and some not so fabulous ones too!

We had wonderful holidays, our own swimming pool, ponies and lived in a lovely big house. Dad even had his own chauffeur and private jet. It lasted long enough to impact on my life in the formative years and created some interesting beliefs too. (More about that later).

Dad unfortunately lost it all overnight and everything turned upside down. It was a very traumatic time and seeing my dad in such a mess was very distressing. It was scary as an 8-year-old child as everything felt threatened.

Luckily we didn't lose the house but lots of other things went. The purse strings became very tight and we went from having what we wanted to having to be, as my mum often said, "very careful".

I am sharing this as growing up is where many of our limiting beliefs are created. I know I certainly adopted my parents for way too long. We all do. Parents can be the best parents in the world but they have their own stories i.e. beliefs and we just adopt them. Some serve us really well and some not.

Experiencing both ends of the money scale has left some impact and some serious clearing and creating new beliefs had to be done. I also was picked on and bullied at school as we had more than most, this created more beliefs that money would never make me happy. All I wanted to be was like everyone else, live in a normal house, drive an old normal car and do what everyone else was doing. Like all children I wanted to be like my peers.

So moving on to becoming a fully functioning adult my dreams did in fact come true. I met and married my husband and lived my dream of being married with children and being a real housewife and stay at home mum. I totally manifested what I wanted, even if it was subconsciously back then as I had not awakened from my spiritual snooze.

My husband and I lived in an ex-council house, drove a Mondeo and never had two pennies to rub together – so I was like most others on the street and my 8 year old beliefs had well and truly come true. Shame that as an adult I no longer wanted to be broke but that is what my mindset believed so I totally manifested financial hardship and when we divorced some years later, we didn't fight over money, we fought over debt!

However, I have a wonderful daughter and son who are both now grown up and living fabulous lives they too have manifested. I have no regrets about anything, as I truly believe everything is teaching us something, especially the difficult things in life. I just wished I had learnt about manifesting sooner.

One of the darkest periods in my life was my divorce, the relationship lasted 10 years and I was left as a single mum with a four year old and a one year old.

It was my worst nightmare, as all I wanted was to be married with children. It was a very scary time and I was consumed with fear. My dreams had ended of being married and my, little family was torn apart. I had a new life to build and whilst at the time I wasn't sure how I was going to get through it, I am here to tell you I did.

I now look back on this time, as a huge turning point and a big blessing, as within all the dark days I found not only my Angels, but myself.

Whilst I have been psychic all my life this is when my development really started. In my desperation I asked for help and my Angels answered. For more on this please see my first book - Do I have an Angel? See link in Chapter 14.

I found a job at Social Services and started to rebuild my life. Not an easy journey by any means and I found myself in debt more times than I care to remember. Each time I maxed out my credit cards I remortgaged my house to clear it again. We were not living a lavish lifestyle but just getting by on one wage.

I wanted more for me and the children. I wanted to be able to say "YES, let's do it", not "we can't afford it". I also wanted to be a stay at home mum again as I hated putting my kids in kids' club and not being able to do the school runs, even though my parents were fabulous at helping out.

One day I was sat in a traffic jam in my home village of Windermere and saw a Bed and Breakfast for sale. My mind wandered to how that would be a wonderful way to provide for my children and earn more money and the best bit was that I would be a stay at home mum again.

This was the turning point, it was the inspiration I needed and something ignited in me. I looked into it and in my heart I knew I could make it work and I could feel my Angels guiding me.

I researched and found a place I could afford. I put my home up for sale and sold anything I had of value to raise the money I needed.

I found a buyer for my home and my offer on the Bed and Breakfast was accepted. It wasn't ideal as the owner's accommodation only had two bedrooms and there were 3 of us, but we were all excited and the children and I agreed we would make it work.

My Angels were working their magic and I was implementing the Law of Attraction by following my simple manifesting practices, it was all coming together perfectly. The sale was going through wonderfully, until that day! I remember so clearly when we were in IKEA buying things for the Bed and Breakfast and the estate agent called to say my buyer had pulled out!

I was there buying things for our new venture and it had all collapsed from under me. I couldn't believe it and didn't know what to do. I stood in the IKEA car park and sent an SOS message to my Angels. I asked them to help so this could all still happen and we could get our new life that we all so desperately wanted.

I felt my guidance like a lightning bolt, it was so strong. In the first moment I was excited as I knew it was the Angels answering me. Then, tuning in more, I understood their guidance I was to call the Bed and Breakfast owners. I felt crushed in that moment, and even more disappointment hit. In fact if I am honest I even felt a bit angry. Was this the best the Angels could do? Why would they tell me to call the Bed and Breakfast's current owners? How ridiculous, of course I had to call the owners, why were my Angels telling me that? I thought they were telling me to just call it all off and I thought my dreams had ended.

We got back in the car and trying my best to hold it all together. I made the dreaded phone call. What actually happened is they were so keen to get out of the Bed and Breakfast trade they offered to buy my house. Incredible, it was all back on again and we were going to do a house swap! I still get goosebumps to this day about that.

I couldn't believe it but of course it was going to happen. The Angels were taking care of it, to think I had doubted them! I did feel a little guilty for thinking badly but I know the Angels don't judge us. To be honest that was the last time I ever doubted the Angels again. They always deliver and work for the highest good of all.

So before long we had moved in and the new chapter of our lives began. The business went from strength to strength and I was booked out each weekend and had a steady fill of rooms in the week, because of course I was using all I knew about manifesting.

It was perfect for us. I was a stay at home mum again and we didn't have any more money worries. It was perfect for a couple of years, well that was until I got ill!

I have had asthma since being pregnant with my daughter and have been in and out of hospital with it, but one day I had a big attack that put me back in hospital and consumed 6 months of my life.

I became allergic to my dogs, dust and various other things, everything was triggering me and my Specialist said if I didn't address all my allergies I might not come out of another attack.

This was yet another dark period that my Angels handled brilliantly. It was incredibly worrying as not only did we have to re-home my 3 little dogs, which was devastating for me and the children, but I also had to find a new income for us all as I could no longer run my Bed and Breakfast, plus find a new home too!

Again, this dark period turned into a huge blessing. In my 6-month recovery period I couldn't do much else but sit around as I was so breathless. My parents and teenage daughter were fantastic and stepped in to do the day-to-day running of the Bed and Breakfast for me whilst I recovered.

All this sitting around meant I had lots of time to meditate and that is exactly what I did. My spiritual development went through the roof. My connections went crazy and the guidance I got freaked me out with its clarity. You couldn't make it up. It was so crystal clear and so easy to put into action there was no doubt this is what I should be doing - my hobby was to become my full time job.

You see I have come to learn that with manifesting when something is right it flows so easily, but if you are hitting snags you need to look at whether you really want something or not. The snags may indicate you are not moving in the right direction.

I have to say I hit no snags. Spirit told me to open a shop and offer my readings that I have done for friends most my life.

I had paid for many a night out doing palm readings in pubs when I was younger and my family and friends have always come to me for spiritual guidance.

The guidance was so clear, I was also told which premises it was, what to sell and even what to call it. It was so crystal clear. I went and viewed the property with my trusty pendulum and it all confirmed it was correct. Not sure what the landlady thought about me doing that, but I knew it was time to step fully out of my spiritual closet and so I couldn't be worried about what others thought, I had work to do.

I had a new business to build, children to support and most of all my gifts to share with the world.

Mystic Moon opened less than 2 weeks from viewing the shop for the first time, even though I had no idea where to source any stock or equipment from. Every time I Googled anything I found it straight away and it was always in stock.

I couldn't mistake this as anything but signs of going in the right direction.

I sold my Bed and Breakfast and moved into a little cottage across the road from the shop so I could keep an eye on my children. It was perfect and the start of yet another wonderful chapter in my life.

I have never regretted opening my Mystic Moon business back in 2009, even though opening a spiritual business in the middle of a recession might have seemed like madness to others. It was very slow at first, but has evolved and grown steadily ever since and now is predominately online. It has supported me and my children, helped thousands of others and still lights me up like a Christmas tree allowing me to share my gifts with this world.

Whatever may come your way in life, my hope is that you get what you need from reading this book and like me can look back on your difficulties as great blessings. So try my practices, experiment and play with the Universe because it is a whole lot of fun when you do.

I hope you learn to be a master manifester like me and my children are and that you create a wonderful life for you and yours.

When it comes to manifesting creating a good solid daily manifesting practice is vital. Try all the exercises out, see what is a fit for you. The idea is not to do everything but find what works for you so you can have some really good manifesting practices every day, then some more tools that you can go back to when you feel stuck or blocked. It has to fit in with your life and there are lots of things you can do whilst you are doing something else like cleaning up, commuting to work, exercising or walking the dog.

For this to work it is about holding your energy in alignment with what you want, so you need to do the inner work daily. Everything I teach fits into busy lives, so don't be giving yourself excuses that you don't have the time to do this. This is you just getting in your own way. You are naturally manifesting anyway, often at an unconscious level so that is how we manifest what we don't want. When you start to do it consciously you become a powerful manifester.

You also need to know that once you have manifested one thing, there will always be something else you want to manifest. It is a continuous journey that should be fun along the way. Not just when you have your manifestation. Some things will be super easy to manifest and others you will feel blocked and stuck with. We all do from time to time. This is perfectly normal, we all fall off our manifesting wagon from time to time, I just want you to know before we start this journey together. Don't worry I will be sharing how you can get back on it too.

Your fears will come up, but that is good as they show you are moving forward. If you stayed in your comfort zone you wouldn't have any fears. Embrace them, give yourself time and use the tools I am going to share.

Extra Resources

There are some extra resources you can download on my site to help you, please see Chapter 14, where you can download meditations like Meet Your Guardian Angel & Manifesting with Your Angels.

A little tip

Think of manifesting as a dance with the Universe. When you first learn to dance it might feel uncomfortable, tricky, hard to remember the steps. You might stumble, trip and fall, but if you keep dancing it will become easier, fun and feel like second nature, it's amazing.

Your Angels will support you too on this journey, so don't forget to ask them as we make our way to your dreams coming true.

The best way to use this book is to read through it once. Don't feel overwhelmed it won't take you too long as many of the exercises you will be able to fully go over when you come to do them.

The purpose of this book is to help you create a successful daily practice that will lead to successful manifesting. That is also what I teach in Abundance Club – my monthly membership site where I share The MAP – Manifesting Abundance Process.

A good solid daily practice will hold your energy in place, it will keep you in alignment with your dreams and desires so you can manifest easily.

The important thing about a daily practice is:

1. It is done daily
2. It is a practice so it may well take a bit of practise for you to get so that it becomes second nature.
3. It fits into your daily life and feels good. If it feels like a hassle or a chore it is creating the wrong energy and needs to be changed.

There are many ways to stay in alignment with what you want to manifest. You just need to find what works for you. Within this book I am sharing lots of ways for you to try. Not just alignment exercises but also things to do when your mood drops off, or as I call it things to *"Flip Your Funk"* and importantly how to feel more connected and supported by the Universe and your Angels.

Once you have read through all the book I suggest you create your own daily practice that works for you and fits into your daily life, no matter how busy you are. This way you will always stay on track with your manifesting and be a master manifester just like me!

I know you will be keen to delve into this book but remember this frequently asked question as you allow yourself to absorb what I am sharing with you.

How do I order from the Universe?

You place your order with your vibration.

Your vibration is made up of your words, thoughts and your feelings.

So you always get what you focus on.

Don't forget to read all the Inspirational True Manifesting Stories in Chapter 13 to inspire you to manifest too.

Contents

Chapter 1

The Universe & What You Need To Know

Your Guide To The Universe
Working With Law of Attraction
Talk The Language The Universe Understands
Commit To Your Dreams

Your Guide To The Universe

Keep remembering we are in this amazing abundant Universe that has the ability to deliver you whatever you want. It has an infinite supply of everything. Everything is energy, everything you want is energy, we are energy.

Where have we come from?

We came from spirit, we are spirit and we are all connected. We can all receive guidance for ourselves and should do every day to feel fully supported. When we start to connect and feel the support Spirit can give us we start to feel an ease and flow in our lives.

It feels like they are rolling out the carpet for us to glide down. We are spiritual beings who have a human reality this time round. When you were born you were a fully connected soul, already able to manifest whatever you wanted. As time moved on you became "humanized" and your spiritual connection got suppressed as human life took over. The wonderful thing is you can reawaken that connection to source energy anytime you like by slowing down, going within and really listening to the whispers of your soul. You will not hear them when you are racing along at one hundred miles an hour.

Who are "The Upstairs"?

We all have Angels assigned to us. You might want to call them something else and that is absolutely ok. I am going to give you a quick overview on Angels and "The Upstairs" as they will help you with your manifesting, but if you want to learn more check out my first book - Do I have an Angel?

Angels are heavenly beings, messengers from Source. They are neither he nor she. You might feel yours is more of a male or a female energy and refer to them as he or she.

Angels are probably one of the few things that all world religions agree on. I don't personally think of my Angels as a religious thing, more of a belief and a connection to source energy, whoever you believe that to be. They are the vibration of unconditional love. They help massively with the internal stuff, giving you strength and the ability to cope with what comes your way in life as well as help you manifest.

When you connect with your Guardian Angel, you always have someone to talk to. You can tell your Angel honestly how you feel — really pour your heart out and get it off your chest. It comes as no surprise to them because they know you inside out. They have been with you since forever and will be with you till forever. All your lifetimes.

Your Angels ask you to give them your problems and all your concerns. When you do, you will find that you can cope more easily. Don't think you will have no more problems, but your ability to cope with them will be far greater.

Everyone has Guardian Angels, at least one! They are your guards and they keep you safe. They have higher vibrational energy than Spirit and have not been on the earth.

It is most important to remember they can't help unless they are asked.

I often think that this is sometimes the hardest bit — remembering to ask because sometimes we (me included) get wrapped up in life and forget to ask. But you should think of them as your first point of call — your first emergency service if you like.

There is only one exception to this rule and that is that they may intervene if it is not the time for a person to pass. So they may well come and save the day if you have a brush with death. We probably all know someone who has come out of a car accident and said "I don't know how I got out of that alive". You can tell when that happens as it is almost like the Angels slow down time and a real calmness comes over the situation.

Your Angel's energy will feel very different from your loved ones in Spirit or your Spirit Guides. To me it feels very light, floaty, soft but dependable, gentle but strong, and most of all a real sense of being loved and cared for. Like nothing I have ever experienced before. To be honest the English language is very limited in finding words to describe them as often they are indescribable.

Whether you see your Angels or not, you will still be able to experience them as they use all our senses to communicate with us.

Angels hear every thought, emotion, wish or prayer you have and they always answer you... even if you may not feel it initially.

We just have to trust and believe. It is also important to say thank you.

The key to working with Angels is to open your heart and your mind to the magic of Angels and then you can receive support and blessings beyond your wildest dreams!

Working With Law Of Attraction
(Rather than against it)

Manifesting with your Angels, Cosmic Ordering, Working with the Law of Attraction are all working with the same Universal Energy. It is creating with energy. It really can be as easy as thinking about something and it happens – I like to think of it as magic and magic is everywhere waiting to turn up for us all the time. I say can, as you will come to see sometimes we 'can' get in our own way and totally block ourselves at times.

For me I have a huge knowing that the Universe will always look after me, but I also like to ask my Angels too as they are so good at the inner stuff. I also know that by manifesting with the Angels they won't get me asking for something I don't feel I deserve, and will also support me when I'm waiting for my delivery.

Life is meant to be joyful, harmonious, fun and filled with love. You have created your life as it is today, whether you realize it or not. And you have the control to turn your life into whatever you want it to be. The Universe delivers ALL your requests, it has your back, you are totally taken care of.

Your requests are actually based on your beliefs. The Universe responds to your energy all the time. This is why people who are having difficult periods in their lives think well "I wouldn't have manifested that". The fact is they have, on some level based around their beliefs as we are always manifesting.

5

We are complex beings and often put restrictions on ourselves, we have limiting beliefs . However, the good news is we also have the power to change it. We even focus on what we don't want, worrying is a prime example of that.

The past does not matter for manifesting, the now is what is important. Working in the now with positivity will allow the Universe to deliver all you want. You need to take control of your manifesting power and that is what we are going to do. One page at a time.

So within this book we are going to heal and clear what is standing in your way. Put in place new conscious manifesting practices and make them part of everyday life, so it becomes second nature.

Some of this may seem difficult at first, uncomfortable, or you may even think - I do this anyway. But I ask you to look really carefully at each step and be really honest with yourself. It is not just a case of doing it for a couple of days and expecting life to change in an instant, to get big lasting changes will take an adjustment in your overall vibration as that is what is always manifesting. Turning yourself into a high vibe magnet will allow you to manifest more positive things and things you really desire.

In simple terms what you focus on becomes your reality. Positive attracts positive and negative attracts negative. But it isn't really as simple as being positive.

When I had my shop if I sold one Guardian Angel I would sell 5 in a row. Same with Angel cards or incense. That was because I was focusing on that one product so more sales happened. We can all probably think of things we have runs of, even if it is a negative thing, like things breaking all the time. Your kettle breaks, then the toaster, you can guarantee something else will because you focus on it and manifest it. How many times have you said things break in threes? What you expect you get!

Stay positive and concentrate your thoughts and feelings on what you want and you will get more of it. So ignore what you don't want, as I am sure you don't want more of that. Remember it is Law......Law of Attraction and the Universe has to deliver whatever you order, i.e. what you focus on.

You can also confuse the Universe by sending mixed messages, this is why it is so important to have head and heart in harmony.

Everything I share in this book can be used to manifest in any area of your life. How you do one thing, is how you do everything. The three examples I will be using are based on the things most people want to manifest, love, health and money. Most other things can be bought with money. However, you can adapt the process around your own personal desires.

The Manifesting Manual

Talk Language The Universe Understands

Imagine for a moment that the Universe is the best department store ever. You can have whatever you want from this store, it's fully stocked ready to go and even does home delivery.

You place your order with this store with only your feelings. If you feel stressed and worried but want to order peace and harmony you get more stress and worry. So your head does not come into this, it is your feelings which create the vibration that the Universe delivers against.

If you want financial abundance but feel broke more bills will come flying through your letter box. You get more of what you focus on.

Can you see how your manifesting could easily go wrong? Well, don't worry I am going to show you how you can turn this around. I just want you to see where you have been getting it wrong till now.

The speed at which your delivery comes depends on how much you believe it, by believe I mean really trust and believe it is coming by keeping your energy aligned. I will teach you exercises as having a daily practice allows you to hold your energy and belief in place. The more you believe the faster it will come to you. HOW your manifestation will come to you is not your job and honestly this is one of the biggest blocks people have.

The HOW it comes to you is the job of the Universe. This is where many people trip themselves up, they decide what they want, then they decide how the Universe can send it to them. They are that focused on that way they can't see the other opportunities the Universe has given them. So they miss their signs and their manifestations because they have their blinkers on.

We have all fallen into the trap of thinking we know better than the Universe. It's crazy right, if that were be the case you wouldn't be wanting to read this book and manifest a better life for yourself.

We actually only have three steps to do:

1. **Decide what we want**
2. **Trust and believe it is coming.**
3. **Follow your inspired action to make it happen.**

The rest is down to the Universe to sort out, after all, it has your back.

Think for a moment when you go to a restaurant and order a lovely meal. You don't go into the kitchen and tell the chef how to cook it. You sit and wait looking forward to it arriving in front of you. Manifesting is exactly the same, you don't tell the Universe how to do it, you just trust it will.

9

The other point I want to clear up is that thankfully there is a buffer of time as such. So you can't just think something and it turns up. Don't get me wrong you can manifest really fast and it can almost feel instant but remember it isn't your thoughts that manifest, it's your feelings.

So you are quite safe to have random thoughts, they won't manifest unless you put focus into them and apply feelings. Can you imagine how crazy that would be? Thankfully The Universe only delivers what we truly believe we FEEL we deserve.

Commit To Your Dreams

Make a commitment to yourself now that you will give this your full attention, because you deserve to have the abundance that you want. Give yourself time each day to do the exercises and the inner work. Remember, it all works inside out. Do the inner work and your outer world will change.

There is nothing more important than how you feel. To do conscious manifesting which is what we are going to do you need to be really clear on what you want. Spend time exploring that. This book is designed to give you a simple process to manifest in all areas of your life so let's get started.

It is so important to know what you really want. Not only that but why you want it and how it will feel. Before you delve into the next chapter I would spend some time thinking about what you want.

You may already really know and if so that is great. Maybe it is a new relationship, job, house move, to start your own business or increase your health, or like many more money.

Don't try and manifest too many things in one go, it spreads your energy too thin. Instead focus on one thing and then when that has manifested you can move on to the next.

It's a bit like spinning plates, get one going and then add another. If you try too many in one go, they all come crashing down and you just get a mess.

If you don't really know what you want and believe me I have worked with many 1:1 clients who always say they don't know what they want. I don't really believe this is the case. It is easy to think that on the surface, but quite often when we don't know what we want, we know what we don't want and that means we are halfway to finding out what we do want.

Another trap people fall into is knowing what they do want but feeling it is too big and almost impossible. So they don't even try to manifest it and settle for something else that doesn't really meet their desires.

The final trip up people make is not feeling worthy and deserving of their desires. This is just old beliefs and the fact you are human means you are as worthy and deserving as the next person. More on that later!

However, denying yourself what you really want, without even trying is less than you deserve. Everyone deserves to feel fulfilled, happy and have what they desire, you included.

Come and tell me what you want to manifest over on my free community (link in Chapter 14).

Chapter 2

Being Open To Receive

Be In Receiving Mode
Things To Do When You're Feeling Blue
Your Natural Default Setting
Your Manifesting Work-Out
Staying Positive

Be In Receiving Mode

I can't stress enough how important this is when you are manifesting. It is often the one step that is missed out of many manifesting approaches that are out there and for me I think it is the most important.

It is about being more allowing. There are two types of thoughts - expansive and contractive. When we have decided what we want we need to hand it over to the Universe to deliver it. We can so easily block it when we think of the lack of what we want. We can feel it is not possible these are all contractive restrictive thoughts. Like wanting more money but feeling broke. Wanting better health but talking about your illness all the time. Wanting a relationship but feeling lonely.

When we have expansive thoughts, there is a sense of excitement and anticipation about it turning up. This will allow you to be in receiving mode.

We can all forget to do this from time to time, life can take over, drama can happen but when that is going on all you will be attracting is more of the same. So the sooner you can turn it around the better.

Often so many fail at manifesting because they are so intensely seriously focusing on what they want to manifest they forget to make it fun. Manifesting is all about the journey and the journey needs to be fun.

Even when your new manifestation has turned up, there will be more things you want to manifest. Trust me, it becomes quite addictive making things turn up for real. I hold my hand up to being addicted to manifesting, it's awesome. So it is never really about the end result but enjoying the journey as you manifest along the way.

Receiving mode is so important, even more important than placing your order with the Universe. Even if you are not clear on what you want if you are in receiving mode you will naturally be attracting good things to you.

If you are not in receiving mode, you will be blocking what you want coming to you, so there is no good placing an order. This is when we are trying too hard and not trusting the Universe enough. We are manifesting from a place of fear.

It is all about fun, doing things you enjoy. Things that make your heart sing.

When you are in the state of joy you can't block anything, you can only attract more joy and abundance to you in all forms. When we manifest, what turns up for us is what we are feeling.

Our feelings go out into the Universe and get reflected back to us. So if we are feeling stressed about manifesting more money, even though we are trying not to we are going to block the money coming.

If we are relaxed and having fun when manifesting the money the vibration going out and, importantly, being reflected back is joy so more money will flow.

So to manifest what it is you want make sure you are having fun doing it, as that is what life is really about.

Laughter really is the best medicine - "When you are laughing you are allowing". Your manifesting won't go far wrong if you adopt this in your life. Now you have probably worked out why I laugh so much.

Check in with yourself have you laughed today? If you have not laughed what made you smile?

What is fun for you? Fun doesn't need to mean expensive. It is the day to day things that you enjoy. It could be spending time with friends, or could be having time for yourself and a bubble bath.

It could be cooking. It could be going for a walk. Doing something creative. Music – Kitchen discos are one of my favorites. There are no rules just make sure every day you are having fun of some type.

As I said earlier try out all the things I suggest go with what feels right, remember if it feels a hassle best do something else that feels more fun. After all, fun is what life is about and it is important to be high vibe energy as much as possible.

Fun Things To Do When You're Feeling Blue

I don't like to leave this down to chance. I take my receiving mode quite seriously (in a fun way of course) and make sure I have things in place to lift my mood when I need to.

I have a list of things to do when I am feeling blue. I write it at the front each time I start a new journal, along with my daily practice. That way it is somewhere I can find it easily when I am off track.

It is totally normal for us to have moods that go up and down, hormones, energy shifts, things can upset us, knock us off the track that is life – and the sooner we get back on track the sooner that our manifestation will arrive.

So when we are consciously manifesting it is important to be aware of how we feel all the time. This is about being at the cause end of life and not the effect. I find this really empowering and means my inner victim (yes, we all have one) has to take a step back. I try to be in receiving mode as much as possible. Think of it as getting into a positive bubble and staying there as much as you can.

When we are feeling blue it is easy to go with the slump in energy and have our little "pity party". I appreciate that sometimes we need to process and work through something. Or there might be something upsetting happening that we need to deal with. Whatever is going on in my life I always try and look for the positive. I reflect what this is teaching me, or what I am re-remembering as often the case is.

However, with general up and down moods I personally like to set an intention that in 2 hours or by the next morning I will be out of it and I will have "flipped my funk".

Exercise – *Things To Do When Feeling Blue*

Make yourself a list of things to do when you are feeling blue. Make sure it is in an easy accessible place.

Having a list of things to do when the blue mood hits means you can refer to it easily. This is so much better than thinking in that moment "what can I do?" as you will probably feel stuck and have no idea. So it means you can pull it round faster and get back to your happy receiving mode again.

Things I like to do when I am feeling blue are:

- Play my uplifting music
- Swim
- Walk by the coast
- Cuddle the dog or children
- Go in my hot tub
- Take a drive out
- Meditate
- Look back at my gratitude journal
- Talk to a friend
- Watch my favourite movie
- Journal

I am sure there are lots of things you could have on your list and I would love to see your lists in my free Community Group (link in Chapter 14).

Tip – If you've still not flipped your funk!

If I have done all the things on my list of things to do when I am feeling blue and my mood still hasn't shifted I personally allow myself to go to bed and sleep it off, but setting the intention that when I wake I will wake in a positive and more uplifted mood.

I hope you have now understood the importance of fun and how it makes a difference to your manifesting. Keeping high vibe energy as much as you can will mean you will attract more good things to you.

Your Natural Default Setting

We are learning to be conscious manifesters. The fact is we are all natural born manifesters and you have been doing it from day one, as naturally as you have been breathing, but on a subconscious level. Manifesting becomes very powerful when you do it consciously.

When you become a conscious manifester it becomes a very powerful tool to create the life you want.

To be conscious you need to be more aware of where your thoughts and feelings are going. It is your feelings that the Universe responds to, but your feelings start with a thought.

Start to be aware of yourself more, are you more of a *Negative Nelly* or a *Positive Polly*? If you are a *Negative Nelly* and are always thinking things are going to go wrong, you are expecting problems, you moan and complain a lot, you have to ask what this is going to manifest? It certainly puts you at the effect end. You will blame others for how you feel. They did this, so I feel that. You are not going to be an empowered manifester from that place.

If you are a *Positive Polly* you are taking charge and this is really empowering. You are at the cause end of whatever happens in life and you choose how you feel. If something triggers you (which is normal) you look at why and heal that issue. If you are naturally upbeat and can see the positives even in difficult situations, you will look at what life is teaching you, what you are learning, what the lesson or the gifts in all situations. You will also be a powerful manifester knowing you create your own reality from the inside out.

Exercise – *Be Aware Of Your Feelings!*

Set an alarm and tune into yourself 6 times a day, to see where you are at. Are you more *Positive Polly* or *Negative Nelly*?

You can take this one step further if you wish and become more aware of the emotions you are feeling and note them in your journal. See if they are more positive feelings like: excited, joyful, confident etc. Or more negative like bored, frustrated, angry, sad, worried etc.

Remember, how you feel is the vibration you are giving out and what the Universe is delivering against.

Knowledge is power with this and if you struggle to think of your emotions it can be a block in your manifesting as just using the word "happy" is too vague.

If you can imagine for a moment you are the Universe and you get an order for someone for happiness, would you know what to send? No, neither does the Universe so clarity is key.

Don't worry, in the next chapter I will help you with identifying more feelings.

Your Manifesting Work-Out

Conscious manifesting does take a bit of practice. Have you ever noticed how sometimes you can manifest somethings but not others. Often we can do the little things like get a parking space then fail miserably at the bigger stuff that we really want.

It is all about your beliefs. You probably believe parking spaces for example are easy to find, so there is no pressure. Let's face it, it's great if you get that ideal parking space but it's no biggy if you don't. So the energy behind it is relaxed and therefore you trust it will happen.

However, when you have something bigger to manifest, like a job, relationship or more money.

There is more pressure. With that pressure can come less belief, so it can end up not happening if you are not careful. You are often focusing on the lack of it too, rather than trusting it is coming.

This is what we think, it's our belief and it is getting in our way. However, to the Universe it makes no difference whether it is a parking space, job, relationship or money.

The Universe knows it can deliver anything as long as it gets your message. Your message is delivered to the Universe by your feelings and beliefs, which is the vibration.

So as long as you believe it enough, it will happen. After all, this is an abundant Universe we are in, even if at times for you it doesn't feel it.

21

You can build your manifesting muscle and get confident with your manifesting results by practise. I like to build my manifesting muscle by daily random manifestations.

I might manifest hearing a certain song, someone making me a cuppa, or someone else putting the rubbish out, seeing a feather on a walk, seeing a purple car on my journey or manifesting someone else cooking dinner or being gifted a lovely bunch of flowers. To be honest it can be anything of little or no importance. It is a game I play with the Universe and it helps me keep my manifesting on point.

It gives me such a buzz and puts the biggest smile on my face when what I manifested turns up and it works my manifesting muscle so I have more belief in my manifesting ability. My addiction to manifesting is satisfied with these little manifestations, they honestly light me up and remind me how magical this world we are in really is.

Plus, I think if I can do purple cars, roast dinners or a random bunch of flowers etc. I can do anything, so my manifesting confidence grows.

One morning as I was tidying up I thought I would love to have flowers in my home, as I hadn't had any for a while. I visualized them where I normally have them and a couple of hours later there was a knock at the door.

My mum was stood there with a beautiful vase of flowers picked from her garden for me. Now I am not saying you initially will manifest as quickly as I do, but you might if you believe enough. Anything is possible as long as you believe it is.

Exercise – *Work Your Manifesting Muscle*

Why not test it out? I recommend you start right now and see how many butterflies you can bring into your reality today.

They don't have to be real butterflies, they can be pictures, photos, wallpapers, anything you like. Enjoy working your manifesting muscle.

Please come along to my free community and let me know how many you manifested in 24 hours (link in Chapter 14).

Staying Positive

Conscious manifesting requires us to stay as positive as possible. I have created myself some rules that help me stay in my positive bubble. Feel free to use them as they are, or to base your own on them. There is nothing more important than how we feel, as that is what we will be attracting more of, so here are the rules I follow.

MY RULES

1. Have fun.
2. Laugh more – "when you are laughing you are allowing".
3. Own my own stuff – if people trigger me I look within for the reason why.
4. Don't get involved in things you don't need to.
5. Don't do drama.
6. Focus on what you want.
7. Don't watch the news or TV.
8. Be careful how I spend my time.
9. Only mix with positive people.
10. Censor & limit the time on Social Media, it can be a very negative place.

Exercise – *Your Positive Bubble Rules*

Write your own rules in your journal – they should be things you can commit to that will keep your energy high vibe and positive. Please feel free to share in my Facebook Free Community Group (link in Chapter 14).

Chapter 3

Get Clarity On Your Desires

Why You Need Clarity

The Universe always requires you to be clear on what you want. If you give out mixed signals you manifest confusion as the Universe doesn't know what to send you.

Sometimes there can be conflict between our head and heart. We want one thing but don't feel deserving and worthy of it, so it cancels our order.

You can't just ask for happiness, love, health or a job. You need to be so much more specific than that.

Think of the Universe like an online fulfillment warehouse. If you were making up the orders and you got one from Susan for happiness and a new job would you know what to send? I'm guessing not. Neither does the Universe.

So being really clear on what you want is key to what will turn up. So to help you I recommend you journal. So many don't and they stay stuck so I want to share a few ways you can do this.

Basic Journaling

Often people don't know what to do with a journal so end up giving up before they even start. My Nana used one and every day she would write what the weather was like and what she did.

That was a nice record for her to look back on, but to be used as part of your manifesting and spiritual practices I would suggest you try some of my suggestions below as there is a lot to be gained from journaling. As with all your practice it is about finding what works for you.

Journaling is a versatile thing and can be used in two ways so you might like to invest in two journals. They don't need to be anything expensive or fancy. Just a notepad to keep everything together. You might like to get some mini post-it notes to use as tags to mark pages you return to often too. Journaling is a great way to get to the bottom of things, as you will soon see when you try it out.

By having a separate journal to do the deeper healing work, or just a good old rant to get it off your chest keeps all the energy you are clearing and healing in one place. The other journal can then be clear to be a creative manifesting journal. The energy in the two books doesn't get muddled (as everything is energy).

If you do want to use just one journal you could go front to back for the healing and back to front for the creative for example.

If you are doing healing journaling you might find you want to rip some pages out and burn them safely to release the negative emotions. If so I would keep to just a cheap notepad for this.

Honestly, there are no rules so do what feels right for you.

What I love about journaling is that it is so much more focused than just thinking about things. It gives you more of a connection to your thoughts and feelings. Writing is so much more productive in understanding yourself than typing.

Healing Journaling

The first journal is going to be your healing journal. This is where you work through your stuff and believe me there will be some stuff. It is not about writing what you did that day. Instead I would encourage you to go deep into how you feel.

Something quite incredible happens when you journal. I find it very cathartic. You can sit, ponder and think about an issue and get nowhere with it. You might even find your mind wanders and thinks of other things because it is painful and your mind wants to take you away from that.

When you journal it holds you in that space and it is surprising what comes up. You can start writing about what you think the issue is and end up writing about something totally different but when you reflect back you can see that what you have written about is the root cause of the issue. Bingo, you have got to the bottom of something and are on your way to healing what is holding you back.

Just remember, even if you feel resistant to journaling, give it a go, it is so worth it. If writing is not your thing. You could record your thoughts and feelings, as you would do if you were writing it in a journal, but on your phone voice recorder app then delete the recording to release the emotions. It is all about joining up the dots and getting it out of you, so it can no longer hold you back. Even just talking out loud helps. I do it in the car or house when I am on my own. It is far better than just sitting and thinking about things as they can just fester and never be released so you stay stuck.

I have journaled for years. My son jokes he is going to read my journals when I am no longer here. Both him and I know that is not going to happen because most of them are illegible. Even I can't read them sometimes when I look back at them. I scribble so fast, words join up, letters are missed out, but it doesn't matter, it is the working through stuff that is important. There is not a right or wrong way to do it. It is all about what feels right for you.

Later on we will be dealing with blockages and you might identify a block. If so, you could then write about it in your journal and see what comes up.

You could write 'I don't know why I am blocked' or 'where have these feelings come from' and see what comes up.

Another thing you can journal on is your stories. Think about the main thing you want to manifest. Then look back and think about your money, love or health story. Think of your childhood, what comes to mind?

Or, think about the goal you have, what comes to mind? Are there some fears attached to it? Ask your Angel to help you.

If you feel resistant to even writing about things/your stories, write that in your journal.

'I don't know why I feel resistance to even writing about…………..*'* See where it leads you.

Try one of my suggestions above and come and tell us about it in my free community (link in Chapter 14).

Creative Journaling

I love this and honestly find this is the best way to call in what you want. It is all about writing about what you want as if you already have it.

Let's start with **3 important questions** that will get you clear on what you want.

1. What do you want?

2. Why do you want it?

3. How will it feel when you have it?

You can do this for any area of your life: love, friends, family, work, business, money, spirituality, fun, contribution, home. Or anything else specific.

It will help you be able to give that clear message to the Universe of exactly what you want and the Universe always needs clarity.

Asking for happiness, to be financially free or successful is just not clear enough. It is time to get specific.

Use your journal to get a clear understanding of what you really want, why you want it and importantly how it will feel.

Focusing on how it will feel takes you away from thinking about how it will come to you. This often leaves so many stuck with their manifesting.

People think their job is to work out how the manifestation will come to them. If they don't know how it can turn up they often don't even try, so get end up getting less than they really want in their life.

The HOW something will turn up for you is the job of the Universe and from my experience it can turn up in the most incredible of ways. It is never your job to work it out, so relax and leave the Universe to do its magic.

It is so easy to block and stop yourselves from getting what you want by falling into the HOW trap.

We all do it at times. We think we know best, and think we know how something we want could arrive into our reality.

Maybe you want a new house and you think a lottery win is the way that could happen.

This not the case and can cause us to trip and stumble with our dance with the Universe. It limits it, as we will only be looking and thinking in one direction of how our manifestation will arrive. That could mean you totally miss other ways because you are looking in the wrong direction.

To stay out of the HOW trap. Those three little questions I shared above really will help you. Here they are again for you.

1. What do you want?
2. Why do you want it?
3. How will it feel when you have it?

Once you are clear on that I recommend you write about it often, I like to think about it as writing it into existence.

Each day in my journal I would write what it is like to have what it is you want as if you already have it. The idea is for it to make you feel good and excited about your future manifestation.

Once you are clear on what you want you are on your way to creating a good daily manifesting practice like I teach in Abundance Club. I will share more about that, plus affirmations and visualizations later. This will keep your energy aligned to what you want to manifest.

With journaling like with all of our manifesting practice, it is all about feeling good. I personally like to have a nice fancy journal for creative journaling if I am using the two journal system. I get excited about doing this and love a new journal for each new big manifestation. Though I am a bit of a stationery addict and I love to write.

How You Are Really Feeling

We need to be really specific when manifesting and not use general words like happy, successful etc. For some people it can be difficult to identify the word. The more expansive you can be the better, so here are some words below to help you.

You can use them in your journaling and to create your manifesting practice. Of course you might have your own too, just make sure they are positive.

Accomplished	Fortunate
Adored	Free
Appreciated	Freedom
Attractive	Fulfilled
Blessed	Important
Calm	Inspired
Comfortable	Loved
Confident	Overjoyed
Content	Passionate
Delighted	Peaceful
Desired	Relaxed
Easy	Respected
Elated	Satisfied
Excited	Tenacious
Flow	Thankful

Chapter 4

Focus On What You Want

Setting The Intention
Mantras
Monthly Intentions
Word Of The Year

Focus and clarity are so important when it comes to manifesting. We can so easily spend our time thinking about problems and worrying, which of course just attracts more of what you don't want into your life. So by learning to set intentions it will help keep your focus on what you want.

Intention setting is like setting a goal, it helps you align your energy. Makes you become more conscious of what you are working towards. There are many ways you can set intentions.

Setting The Intention

Each day as I wake in my sleepy state, one of the first things I do is I set an intention of something I want to achieve, be or manifest that day. It might be to have fun, feel calm, connected, achieve a task, or manifest something specific.

Setting intentions, are one of the ways you can place your order with the Universe. You can do it anytime not just as you wake but as you are going through your day.

For example:

- Set the intention to be ready for work on time.
- Set the intention for a safe and congestion free journey.
- Set the intention to complete a task by a certain time.
- Set the intention to have an enjoyable lunch with a friend.
- Set the intention to get clear on what you want to manifest, which is particularly useful if you are feeling a little confused.

Mantras

According to Deepak Chopra the word mantra can be broken down into two parts: "man," which means mind, and "tra," which means transport or vehicle. In other words, a mantra is an instrument of the mind—a powerful sound or vibration that you can use to enter a deep state of meditation.

Mantras increase your awareness and bring focus into your life.

You can use them in meditation or within your daily practice. Personally I like to write mine on post it notes so I can see them and remind myself of them daily.

My current one is – *I can and I will!*

Other mantras you might like to use are:

- I am more than enough.
- I am beautiful and strong.
- I am attracting abundance and prosperity.
- I am perfect as I am.
- I am fulfilled and fearless.
- I am financially abundant.
- I am abundant in all ways.
- I have all the time I need.

Of course feel free to create your own depending on what you want to work on and improve within yourself.

Monthly Intentions

Each month within my private manifesting club – Abundance Club – I do a live intention setting session. This is important to get clear on what you want for the coming month so you can craft your daily practice around it.

Spend a few moments thinking about the different areas of your life and how satisfied and in control you feel about each one. Grade them out of 10. 1 being low and 10 being the highest.

- Home
- Work/business
- Money
- Health/body
- Social life
- Friends
- Pets
- Money
- Holidays
- Car/transport
- Relationship
- Time off
- Fun
- Spirituality
- Family
- Creative
- Contribution
- Anything else

Some of the areas might not be relevant to you, they are just ideas. Feel free to make your own list.

Wherever you are, remember, this is just a starting place. It is something to work on, some might be high, some much lower, there is no right and wrong, it is just where you are now and it will give you an indicator of what is the most important to change first.

When you start to do your manifesting by having a daily practice in place things can change very quickly.

When we are manifesting it is a good idea not to try and change everything in one go. Instead work on a maximum of 3 things and when they have changed you can move on. It will get you much quicker results this way round.

Then re-check each month and see how things are going, what needs more work and what is turning out perfectly. You never want to spread your energy too thinly, that weakens your manifesting power.

Word Of Year

Having one word for the year that is your focus and that can refer to many areas of your life is something I recommend everyone does.

Each year I like to pick a different word and watch how that manifests and ripples through my life.

Some of the more recent ones have been:

LOVE – it became my focus to only do what I loved, and if I didn't love something I reflected if I needed that in my life. If it was things like the washing up, I asked myself how could I love it more. Putting music on whilst doing it was an easy fix.

EASE – when I picked this word I went from working 6 days to 3!

You can pick any word, here are some more to help you:

- Confidence
- Joy
- Fun
- Health
- Contentment
- Forgiveness
- Success
- Unbound
- Limitless
- Freedom
- Unstoppable

So what is going to be your word of the year? Don't wait for a new year to come round to pick one, do it now whatever date it is. Think of it in all areas of your life.

Chapter 5

Your Daily Practice Part 1

Your Daily Practice

This is where it is starting to get exciting, but I want to warn you that you can't create a successful daily practice unless you know what you want. So don't try and delve straight in here if you haven't spent some time getting clear on what you want. It is something you are going to do each day to hold your energy in alignment with what you want. It is really important for it to feel good and not a hassle or a chore. Make it fun.

Creating Your Daily Practice

In the last chapter I spoke about focus and you can certainly bring your mantra into your daily practice to give it more focus, I totally recommend that. However, we really need to hold your energy in alignment to your desires and I like to think of Affirmations and Visualizations as belt and braces to your manifesting that will do exactly that. They change your vibration so you focus on what you want and by doing that you will manifest.

Your daily practice should always feel fun and fill you with excitement as you know it is bringing to you what you want. If it feels like a chore and a drag you need to change it as ultimately that is the energy you are vibrating so you will just attract more of it.

Your aim is to come out of your daily practice feeling good. If you aren't please address that and tweak as needs be.

I love doing my daily practice. It fills me with joy and anticipation for what is coming.

You are aiming to create a good spiritual and manifesting practice that you commit to daily, so you can see your results fast. It doesn't need to take a lot of time and most things can be fitted around other activities. In fact, I would always say make sure they do if you can.

Affirmations are more powerful if you do them whilst you are doing something else. It could be exercise, walking the dog, commuting to work or even doing chores around the house. The same with many types of visualizations. So when you have created your own affirmations I recommend you record them on your phone so you can listen to them and make good use of your time. Let's face it we are all busy people.

I know some of you will say I hate the sound of my own voice. So did I to start with, but you get used to it. Did you know that with your unconscious mind there is nothing more powerful than your own voice? So even if we were working 1:1 and I was creating your affirmations and visualizations for you I would still get you to record them. I guess the big question here is: are you going to let your dreams slip by because your voice makes you feel a little uncomfortable? If so you have to question how much you really want change in your life.

Your daily practice is called a daily practice because you do it daily and you need to practise it! Simple really. The reality is it can soon be skipped, you wake up late, miss a bit here, miss a bit there and next thing you are not doing it and then you say your manifesting is not working. Well, it won't be as you need to question what your focus has been on.

What I love within Abundance Club is you can never fall off your manifesting wagon as there are 3 levels of your daily practice – There is the non-negotiable level that you do even if you are running late and having one of those mornings, we all have those sorts of days from time to time. Then there is basic practice you can do most days when life is ticking along nicely. Then there is advanced practice for when you want to manifest something fast or have more time. This means that you never fall off your manifesting wagon so your mindset is always one of success and you will naturally manifest more good things in your life.

For the purpose of this book I am going to share lots of exercises you can use to create a daily practice for yourself. I will give an example of a standard practice that many use, you can base yours on that and adapt as you wish. Of course if you want more support in different manifesting practices like non-negotiable, basic and advanced you will want to access Abundance Club you can go there and find out if we are accepting new members (link in Chapter 14).

Once you have created your own daily practice I recommend you write it in the front of your journal so you can easily refer back to it and keep on track.

You need a morning and evening practice for example:

Morning Practice:

- Set daily intention
- Ground & Protect
- Meditation
- Affirmations
- Visualization

Evening Practice:

- Gratitude
- Journaling
- Visualization

You can make it as short or as long as you need.

Remember you can do everything except meditation or journaling whilst you are doing something else too, so your practice doesn't need to take up a huge amount of time, unless you want them too.

It is so important that it is worth mentioning again, that your practice has to make you feel good. You want to love doing your daily practice, if not, switch it about so you do.

You might want to create a specific place in your home that you do your daily practice. My bedroom is often my go to place. I have created a little altar in there with my Angel Cards, candle, crystals and other bits and pieces that I felt inspired to put together.

The main thing is it works for you and feels good.

Affirmations

There are many ways to stay in alignment and if I was to pick my favourite way it would always be affirmations. Staying in alignment means keeping the end goal at the forefront of your mind as much as possible.

Affirmations are vital to changing your unconscious mind and in ensuring your manifestations turn up.

In fact, they are the only thing that will re-programme your unconscious mind so make sure you give them a real go.

Affirmations are things you say over and over again until you believe them. I joke it is like brainwashing but it really does change the unconscious mind.

They need to be short, snappy sentences that, if you were writing, would be no more than one line long.

They become more powerful when started with "I am……"

As "I am" refers to your higher self, that part of you that is always connected to source energy.

Everything I teach must fit into busy lives and you need to remember that as you craft your new practice. So, don't overcomplicate things as manifesting really is simple.

Affirmations are also best done whilst doing something else, so there is no excuse not to do them. You can just say them out loud or in your head.

You can record them on your phone and listen to yourself repeating them. In fact, listening to them recorded in your own voice works even better.

You can say your affirmations in the shower, whilst doing exercise or chores, walking the dog, driving the car and so on. They are so versatile there really is no end to how they can be done.

I totally recommend you do an action whilst saying them as it absorbs them into your body. I even have mine recorded on my phone and then listen to them as I am getting ready in a morning.

If you are going to record them, record each one for approx. 1 minute before moving on to the next. I would create 10 and then you will have 10 minutes of affirmations to listen to which will change your mindset.

You can even write your affirmations down. Remember when you were at school and you got lines? It is the same thing. You were given lines because if you wrote the sentence over and over again, you would think it and if you thought it you believed it and if you believed it you did it. It is the same with affirmations, and if you believe it, you will see it.

If you choose to write them down, write them for 5 days in a row, 55 times for each day. Be warned though, you get arm ache, but if you want to power up your manifesting I totally recommend you do this but with just one main affirmation. It is a great way to align your energy and give you a boost. Don't be mistaken that after 5 days you will manifest what you want, you might but it will certainly move you a lot closer to it.

Once your manifestation has turned up you will need to tweak your affirmations to the next thing you want to manifest. As believe me, there will always be new things to manifest.

Here are some standard affirmations I recommend and use myself. I use these when I am not sure what I want to manifest or when something comes along that feels like a challenge. I like to remind myself of these and I instantly feel better which is all we ever need to do.

Standard Affirmations

- Everything always works out for me.
- How can it get any better than this?
- The Universe has my back.

Some other affirmations for you to try:

Money Affirmations

- Money comes to me easily.
- Money comes to me in unexpected ways.
- I am worthy of money.
- I deserve money.
- I love money and money loves me.
- Money is my friend and loves to hang out with me.
- I am a money magnet.
- I am easily earning X per month.

Health Affirmations

- I am fit, well and moving with ease.
- I am becoming slimmer and fitter each day.
- I am full of energy and vitality.
- I am healthy, well and loving life.

Love Affirmations

- I am pure love.
- The more love I give, the more love I receive.
- I love others and others love me.
- I am accepting of all love.
- It was easy for me to manifest my new lover.

Time Affirmations

If you are struggling with time, you might like to use these ones. As I know so many of my clients struggle with time.

- Time is abundant.
- Time expands for me.
- I always have more than enough time.

You could put your affirmations on post-it notes around your home.

Change your password on your computer or banking app to your favourite one, so every time you log on you think about the main thing you want to manifest.

Have your main affirmation written in your purse and each time you spend some money you can see it. I must admit, I used to have a picture of the kids as babies in my purse and in fact still do, but now on top of it I have my main goal written as an affirmation.

So, there are lots of ways to do your affirmations I would do them as often as possible, but certainly once or twice a day if you are working on manifesting something important and you want it fast, do them more.

If you travel to work it is a perfect time to do them, then if you feel you need to realign your energy part way through the day you can do them again at lunchtime.

Most of all enjoy them in the knowledge that each time you say one you are one step closer to it manifesting.

Visualizations

Your feelings and emotions are what create your vibration, which is the language the Universe understands. So it's super important for you to be fully aware of them and keep moving them in the direction of what you want, rather than what you don't want.

This is why the feelings are so important with manifesting. Packing out your visualizations with all the feelings and emotions that you believe the manifestation will feel like when it arrives using all your senses is not only fun but vital to the results you will get.

When you realize it is the feeling you are after with your daily practice, this takes the pressure off the manifestation. You can enjoy your visualizing so much because if you become good at it you can't tell if it is real or not. When you get to that place that is when things really start to speed up with your manifesting.

Visualizations are a way of feeling it first and we always have to feel it before it turns up for real.

One of the common questions asked is how you do it?

Do you visualize as if you are experiencing it (associated) or visualize watching yourself experience it (disassociated)? With my eyes open or closed?

It matters not, whichever you prefer. The main thing is that it feels good.

I am not expecting you to do all I suggest in one go.

Just pick and choose one type of visualization that you feel you would enjoy. Try the visualization out, if you want to switch to something else after a week or so do that. Remember with some of these I am going to share you will be able to create them and then record and listen to them on your phone or device. Most phones these days have a voice record app or voice memos you can use.

I think it is much easier to either read visualizations or listen to them on your phone or device as it is so easy to get distracted.

Visualizations are great things to go to sleep listening to, what better than manifesting as you go to sleep, drifting off into your new life.

Permission For A New Life

Whatever you are wanting to manifest, give yourself permission to start being the person you want to be right now. This might feel like pretending at first, but remember it is going to become real soon enough.

So spend at least 5 mins each day pretending to be the person you want to be. So even if you feel like you don't have enough time to sit down for a cuppa and relax, do it! Even if you have not got the ideal job you want, act like you do. Even if you have not got that amazing relationship you want, draw in those feelings it will give you and walk around pretending to be in love.

When I was manifesting a new relationship and was making a cuppa I would shout out and ask him if he wanted one, even though he was not there YET! Sounds crazy I know but you have to feel it first for it to manifest.

Whatever is on your list to manifest act as if you already have it for at least some of your time. By doing this you are creating the energy for it to come to you. It makes the journey more pleasurable as you are waiting for it to come to you. What you feel on the inside is what you manifest on the outside.

The 4 P's

Visualizations must be the 4 P's – Positive, Powerful, Present and Passionate. Don't worry if they are not visually clear in your mind, the main thing is they feel good.

- Use words, sounds, smells, mental pictures and, most importantly, feelings.

- If you see yourself in the visualization pay close attention to every small detail, such as what you are wearing, and whether there are other people in the visualization, don't leave anything to chance.

- Keep practising so that your pictures become clearer in time.

This is so important – otherwise you will have a *manifesting malfunction* and nobody wants one of those!

You will know when you have affirmations and visualizations right, because you will feel relaxed and confident that your manifestation will arrive. I sometimes feel excited and get butterflies in my tummy.

Mini Visualizations

If there is something specific you want like a new job, relationship, new car etc. Just try and think about what you want for 2 mins each time. You can set a reminder if you want. Sometimes it is easier to visualize telling someone you have manifested it.

Do this 2 to 3 times a day or more on exactly that specific thing. The beauty of this is you can do this anytime, when you are sat in traffic or queuing somewhere. Just start visualizing that you have whatever you want now. Don't forget to use all your senses, go into as much detail as you can and really feel it so you get really excited about it.

Big Visualizations

You can do this when you are wanting to manifest more than one thing and turn it into an ideal day visualization.

Exercise - *Ideal Day Visualization*

Step One

Write down what you want to happen in your life. Go big with this - really don't hold back. Think of all areas of your life. As you are writing it down leave a line in-between each line. You can use the journaling exercise from earlier to help you.

Step Two

Once you have written everything you would do in your ideal day, go back to the lines not written on. Write down how it would feel to be doing what you want in your ideal day. Remember feelings are really the key in manifesting.

When you have finished it you will have something like this.

E.g. Ideal day

> *I wake up – in my light, bright, comfortable holiday home overlooking the sea, it is a beautiful sunny day. I wake up refreshed after a good night's sleep with my gorgeous partner lying next to me. He is the most loving, caring, understanding & supportive man I have ever met. I feel so lucky to have found him and in my relaxed dreamy state I look out of the*

window at the sea shining with the sun reflecting off it. Today is going to be amazing, I feel so comfortable and relaxed in my own skin, totally happy with my wonderful life.

I have a delightful breakfast with no hurry, healthy foods. The house is clean and tidy as our wonderful cleaning lady had been in yesterday giving it the once over ready for our stay.

I'm surrounded with family and enjoying their company and getting on so well. We are all chatting about the day ahead. It feels so exciting, secure and exhilarating to have such an amazing life.

I get ready and do my morning routines. My partner pops his head back into the room kisses me goodbye and squeezes me gently. He smells so divine. His touch is so tender, I completely trust him and feel like the most important person to him as indeed he is to me. He is off with the boys to play golf. I love that he has his own interests as it means I have time for mine too.

I spend some time getting ready and doing my daily practice sat in the garden with warm summer sun peeking through the clouds warming my body on the comfortable lounger, listening to the waves roll in.

As I quickly check my emails from my clients, I am overjoyed at reading the emails of people wanting *to work with me. The club has grown so fast, I am helping so many people and my diary is so full now. I have a waiting list of clients. I feel so blessed for work to be this easy, fun and rewarding. I work 3 days per week and spend the rest of my time writing, painting, swimming and have fun with my fabulous like-minded positive friends.*

I'm lovingly interrupted by the squeals of my grandchildren running over the grass, excited to see me, all ready for the day together.

My puppy Millie runs alongside them. I scoop both the children up and snuggle them as they giggle with delight.

We plan our morning, us girls together whilst the boys are all off doing their thing.

A walk on the beach, paddling, making dens in the garden, playing hide and seek and catching up with my daughter as the children play.

Lunch is spent catching up with a friend in a lovely café with sea view. We sit enjoying each other's company, relaxing and putting the world to rights. I love having spiritual friends who really understand you, nothing needs to be explained. We pop into a fabulous crystal shop nearby and I treat myself to a huge citrine crystal to add to my collection and a couple of small pieces for the grandchildren. They just love them like me, they call them treasure.

Later, we are all back home and the family is back together, all enjoying our holiday home and the buzz of high vibe energy. The conversations are always expansive and I adore seeing how well both my son and daughter are doing in their lives, both in business and personally. As we gather round the huge kitchen table chatting about future plans for us all I have a huge sense of pride in how far we have all come.

It is soon interrupted by the excited children looking in the cupboard for the marshmallows ready for after the BBQ. My gorgeous partner is in the kitchen putting together quite a feast. He is such a great cook, and his meals are always so healthy and delightful. It is wonderful as I rarely have to cook these days.

Everyone mucks in and before long we are all sat outside in the evening sun, dogs and children still running round with boundless energy. We sip a gorgeous new wine we have discovered from the local supplier, it is organic and has a fresh orange hint. Our wine tasting course really paid off, we now know what to pick and more importantly what we like.

As all the family make their way to bed, my partner and I take a walk on the beach with the dog running free. One last burst of exercise before the sun sets. The sky is the most incredible colour as almost pulls us in and reminds us what a magical world we are in.

My lovely man, as he does each night, tells me to go up and he will lock up. It is so perfect as it gives me time to do my evening practice before he joins me in bed. He thinks I don't know but he loves the time for him and Milly to have a cuddle. He is such a softy.

He brings her up into our lush bedroom and she settles down in her bed. As we both lie there doing our gratitude practice and chatting, filling each other in with our days. He is a business man too and chats easily about our future plans. He is so good to sound things off against. I love having him in my life. We start discussing our next holiday. We both fancy another cruise, just us adults only.

I can't remember ever feeling so content and happy with life in all ways.

How can it get any better than this?

Of course this is just an example. You can create yours however you like. The main thing is it is what you want and it makes you feel good. It is a nice way of bringing lots of things together without spreading your energy too thin. Notice too I ended it with *How Can It Get Any Better Than This?* It invites even more good stuff in. Rather than saying *it can't get any better than this,* which limits it.

Once you have created your Ideal Day and it makes you feel amazing to read it, you then need to read it twice a day or even better record it and listen to. This is a great one to go to sleep listening to.

Future diary

Most of my clients love this. It is like writing your own future as one day can follow on to the next.

It is like writing a diary. However, instead of what you have actually done, you write what you would have liked to have happened. It often ends up being a mix of what you have done and a few extra tweaks of what you would have liked to have done to make it even better. Like with all visualizations you need to not only say what you have done (or would like to do) but also how it felt.

The incredible thing about this is it doesn't take long to start to happen.

One story I love to share that I hold Future Diary totally responsible for is this....

It was back a few years ago when I went on my first date in years! I had been chatting with a guy who seems nice, he was a farmer and asked to meet. We arranged to meet in a nearby pub late afternoon.

It turned out to be the longest 20 mins of my life. The guy was still nice, don't get me wrong but he came straight off the farm, no washing, no change of clothes and quite honestly he stunk! I had one drink and left! We were not on our own on the date there was a fly who loved his cow muck covered trousers and sat on his leg the whole time!

I can't tell you how disappointed I felt. If this was dating I was not prepared to do it again. If a man couldn't wash for a first date, it was not looking good for future ones.

On my drive home it came to me that I had to be clearer on what I was looking for and I had to work through this disappointment. I could feel the urge to purge it all out in my Healing Journal. Then I realized - no I needed to - create instead. This is when Future Diary was birthed!

I got out my journal and started to write this:

Oh wow, I have just had the most incredible date with a man I felt comfortable with from the start. We went to the local pub and we had a fabulous time. We had an amazing time and he is quite spiritual too. Which was a big bonus for me. He was dressed so smart but casual, smelt divine and you could see he made an effort and took good care of his appearance.

We even like the same food and drinks. He was telling me about what he loves to cook and what things he enjoys. He was so open and honest, there was a real connection that I have not felt for a long time. I was so relaxed in his company and could really be myself.

He was quite the gentleman and really took care of me, I felt valued and appreciated. He was interested in my life as I spoke comfortably about myself. There was no gap in the conversation. We chatted so much, time flew and next thing the pub was closing. Yes, there will be date two. How can it get any better than this?

It doesn't need to be long, just a few short paragraphs, but it has feelings and reinvents your day the way you would have liked it to have gone.

That night I went to sleep not feeling disappointment but excitement. The stinky date was not on my mind, but the dream date was. Two weeks later I went on exactly the date I wrote about.

Future Diary is a fun way of creating your future too. I hope you enjoy it as much as me and my clients do.

Dear Universe Letter

This is such a lovely way to visualize as it brings into it the vibration of appreciation and gratitude.

It is something you can create and then read to yourself twice a day (or listen to if you record it.)

It always makes you feel good because it is based on the attitude of gratitude.

You write a letter to the Universe filled with gratitude and appreciation of what you want as if you have already got it. You must pack it out with emotions (as normal) so just think how it will feel when you have got what you want. It can be about anything you desire, you can do it about just one thing or a few areas of your life, the main thing is it has plenty of gratitude and feelings in it.

E.G.

Dear Universe

Thank you so much. I have a huge sense of gratitude and appreciation for all you have sent me and all you are continuing to send to me.

It feels amazing to wake each morning! After a blissful night's sleep and feel so excited about the day ahead. I am so grateful each day for a new opportunity to experience more magic and the miracles that you are constantly sending to me.

Life is really working out in the most incredible way. I am so appreciative of how easy and flowing it is. I only seem to have to think of something and it manifests.

I feel so fit, healthy and well, my body is working perfectly and I am taking such great care of myself. I have realized my own self-worth and my body is my priority.

I am spending my time so wisely that I always have more than enough of it for all I want to do and I live my life at such a steady even pace.

When I open my wardrobe each day I have so many

wonderful choices of clothes I can choose to wear, which all look incredible on me. I get compliments wherever I go and I feel amazing.

I am feeling so connected and supported in my life, not just spiritually but by those around me too. It feels wonderful to be fully understood and that is because now I understand myself due to investing in myself and getting support with my fabulous coach.

My self and spiritual development has meant I am really on track with my life. Manifesting is now easy because I have clarity about what I want to experience.

It gives me great joy to look at my banking app and see my savings growing, I am so very grateful for all the abundance and prosperity you send me. Money loves to hang out with me and brings its friends. It means I can not only look after myself but my family and friends well too. I am loving being able to support the charities that mean so much to me. Giving back and making a difference to people I don't even know but I know I am helping in some way.

Paying into the wonderful Universe has been such a game changer, I see how the more I give the more I receive in all ways, including gratitude.

I have so much appreciation for my work, it fulfills me and I adore what I am doing, I have such amazing clients who don't mind waiting to see me as I am so booked up. Thank you so much for each and every *one of them they are all a pleasure to work with. Each time I launch something new it fills up to fully booked in no time at all. I am just so blessed with my work and appreciate all aspects of it.*

The biggest thing I have a huge sense of gratitude for is the amazing man you sent me. Wow, he turned up in the most spectacular of ways. How did you know exactly what I was looking for, I shouldn't be surprised but he is wonderful and kind. I guess you knew that is what I needed. Thank you for all you send me, how you always support me, I love the trust I have in you.

How can it get any better than this?

As you can see, I have ended it with *How Can It Get Any Better Than This*? To invite even more magic in.

You can create your Dear Universe Letter about whatever you want. Just make sure you enjoy it and use lots of gratitude and appreciation.

Act As IF - AAI

This is such a great game to play and even better if you can get a friend to play it with you, but you can equally do it on your own. I love to play this with my retreat clients on Angels in Anglesey.

So here is what you do, you talk out loud, saying how amazing life is, talking about what you want to turn up as if it already has.

I sometimes play it in the car on my own, pretend I have my best friend sat next to me and I chat out loud (that's the important bit, not in your head) describing in detail what has happened and how I feel.

If you can get someone to play it with you it makes it extra powerful as they build the energy with you. So when you say something and they respond and you continue the conversation as if it has already happened it becomes a super powerful manifesting tool.

I like to play it on long car journeys, in fact I played it with a friend on the way back from a holiday in Wales. It was such good fun. We were talking about how she sold her home with such ease and moved to Southport to be by the seaside, it all happened so easily and so fast. On the same journey she got a call from the estate agent saying they had a lady wanting to view on Saturday, she was looking for exactly that type of property and was ready to proceed. I said to her that's your buyer and she looked at me with a new twinkle in her eye and said, "Yes I do believe it is".

Needless to say, it was her buyer and she did move fast and easily. It was far different from the conversation we had on the way there, when she was complaining about no one viewing.

I also play it when walking the dog with my friend. Or even in the hot tub with the kids. It all helps our ability to manifest, as what we believe, we receive.

Chapter 6

Your Daily Practice Part 2

Staying High Vibe
Ramp Up Your Manifesting With Gratitude

Staying High Vibe

I am making no apologies to remind you that, gratitude is the only attitude you will ever need.

It really is the fastest way to turn things around. When you are feeling blue and life is throwing some curve balls in your direction, or you have just lost your mojo, getting back to gratitude really helps to turn things around.

We need to remember that however we feel that is what we are manifesting more of. So it is super important to feel just a little bit better if we are suffering with the blues.

Gratitude is a huge game changer and you literally can't feel stressed if you have gratitude. The two emotions are polar opposites.

We all know that once in a while something will catch

our attention, maybe in the media, and make us really grateful for the life we have. The reality is we are often so busy rushing around and we take too much for granted.

Now I say this with love and without judgment but I have noticed a huge difference with my clients. The ones manifesting real magic in their lives are the ones that are always grateful and have a great sense of appreciation. They make a conscious effort to find it.

The ones that moan and complain about their lives are the ones that always have something to moan about and sadly life never seems to get any better for them.

It really is crystal clear that the more we give appreciation and gratitude the more we have to be grateful for and I know which camp I would rather be in, so the bit of conscious thinking each day about gratitude pays off.

I love to write my gratitude each day in my gratitude book. Honestly though, if I am tired I will just think it instead. What I love about a gratitude book is that I can refer back to it when I am wobbling and thinking everything is going wrong and it puts it all into perspective that actually I have a lot more to be grateful for and this is just a blip.

One other thing I love about gratitude is that it is something really easy to suggest to others. Even people who are not really spiritually open seem to be open to gratitude and the difference it can make in their lives is huge. After all, we can't expect to receive more from the Universe if we are not grateful for what we have got already.

When we are manifesting there are two ways to feel about what we want.

1. From a place of lack that it is not in our life. The frustration will just then take over and push what you want further away.

2. From a place of gratitude and anticipation that it is on its way. The excitement will draw it to you even faster.

So be grateful for the penny you find on the street, never walk past it. Pick it up and thank it and appreciate it as money coming to you, then more will keep flowing.

Tip – If you give gratitude for something that hasn't manifested yet it will speed the manifestation up as it strengthens your trust in the Universe.

Ramp Up Your Manifesting With Gratitude

Some exercises for you to try so you can work with gratitude and shift your vibration as you need to are these.

Exercises – *For Gratitude*

1. Daily Gratitude

Doing daily gratitude work means you are keeping your energy high vibe and more good things will flow to you. Each day write a list of at least 10 things you are grateful for. You can do it in your normal journal or in a separate gratitude book. Write your list of everything you can be thankful for today, try and really go deep, mix it up each day so the same things don't keep appearing day upon day. You will find though some regular things come round often, it might be family, pets, chocolate (if you are like me) and that is ok, but as long as there is a good mix of different things within it too.

You could put things like: Being alive, family, friends, home, food, job, love, kindness, smiles, hugs, flowers in the garden, your pets, your favourite cuppa or glass of wine.

I like to do it just before going to sleep. But as with all the exercises, do it whenever it works best for you.

It is great to share gratitude and seeing what others put on their lists helps. So feel free to share your gratitude list in my free community (link in Chapter 14).

2. Super Grateful

If you find that easy I challenge you to find 100 + things to be grateful for. This will really shift your vibration higher.

3. Rolling gratitude

As well as doing a list of daily things to be grateful for, a great way to turn things around is to do rolling gratitude.

This gets you really present and in the moment. The now is so important as this is the place we manifest from so if it feels good you are going to manifest good things.

It requires you to consciously think about everything within the now. E.g. starting your day.

- Grateful for a new day.
- All your senses and your body for the way it works
- Good night's sleep.
- Safety of your home.
- Warm water of the shower.
- Bubbles of the products you use.
- Soft, fluffy towel to dry yourself on.
- Clothes to dress in.
- Moisturiser to smooth into your skin.
- Brush to tidy your hair.
- Tea in your cup, the cup itself, the water, the tea manufacturers.
- The breakfast food you have.
- The shoes on your feet.

I'm sure you get the idea but everything you do, you start to be present and give gratitude for it.

- Your eyes for reading this.
- Your brain for understanding.
- The chair you are sitting on.
- The air you are breathing.
- The chance of another day to experience.
- Your family, your friends, your health, even if it isn't perfect.
- Your finances even if you want more.

If you spend even just 20 minutes doing real conscious gratitude work it will shift your mood. So whilst you are going about your day you are present and giving gratitude for everything in that moment. You can't be low or down or cheesed off when you do this, it seriously makes you feel better and, as I hope by now you understand, it is all about how you feel.

4. Conscious Gratitude

Another manifesting hack you might like to try is based on gratitude too. Get present to this very moment and start acknowledging everything you are grateful for within this moment wherever you are. You can do it with your eyes open or closed but spend 2 minutes really being present and giving gratitude for all you are experiencing in that very moment.

You will notice your energy rising and yourself starting to move to feeling more positive. After 2 minutes, switch your thoughts to the one main thing you want to manifest and feel that high vibe energy. It feels exciting as you are blending the gratitude for the present moment plus gratitude for what is coming and when we give gratitude for what we want to manifest it speeds up its arrival.

I don't recommend you do rolling or conscious gratitude daily but have it in your toolbox of things to do when you need a pick me up.

Chapter 7

Identifying Blocks, Fears & Limiting Beliefs

What Is Holding You Back
Healing Your Stories
Clearing Your Money Blocks
Common Blocks, Fears and Limiting Beliefs

What Is Holding You Back

This is a chapter you will more than likely have to come back to time and time again. The thing is about blocks, fears and limiting beliefs is they are always coming up. Often they need clearing on many levels. Like layers of an onion.

You peel back one layer and feel the shift, life starts moving in the direction you want again. Then boom you are stuck again and you have to clear another layer and go a bit deeper.

It is quite normal, so don't feel bad. We are all work in progress and always have to keep working on ourselves.

So come back here whenever you feel stuck, blocked and held back.

It's often not easy doing this deeper work, so be kind to yourself. I don't say that lightly the process is quite simple, but what it may take you through may be personally tough, either way it is so worthwhile.

Blocks and limiting beliefs are often fear based. This might be the fear of the outcome or lack of outcome, or even the consequence of the outcome in a positive or negative way. Some of these fears may be valid and some may not, but we just think they are, based on past experiences. As what we believe, whether it is true or not, is what we will experience as we believe it is true.

As Henry Ford said:

Whether you think you can, or you think you can't – you're right.

The fantastic thing is, on the other side of fear is exactly what you want. So you are already taking steps to make your dreams come true?

The *past* is behind you, where fears are created, and the *future* is ahead of you, where anxiety lives.

What we have now is the *NOW*. This is the important bit. The now is creating your future.

You might be noticing yourself saying:

- I can't
- But
- It's hard

If so you are exactly in the right chapter and it is great you are aware of that, as what you say, you feel and what you feel you experience. You will get a very different outcome if you swap it to:

- I can
- And
- It's easy, I can do this

Healing Your Stories

The interesting thing with blocks is they will all clear at different levels. If they don't clear after the first thing you go on to the next thing I suggest until you have created a new mindset etc.

The other thing I find fascinating with blocks, fears and limiting beliefs is we all share them. Whatever is holding you back now will be holding someone back too. We adopt other people's blocks and fears and pass them down generation after generation. Some even come from past lives.

Whatever you want to manifest, the main block is always going to be you and what you believe to be true.

I would urge you now to question all beliefs and ask are they really true?

The word belief actually is based on "lie" – Belief. So with limiting beliefs there is a good chance what you believe could well be based on a lie! They are just stories you tell yourself and you can always tell yourself a new story. Limiting Beliefs are unhelpful, unsupportive ideas and beliefs you have about yourself, your sense of self-worth, how much you feel worthy and deserving (or not) of wealth, love, health, happiness and all the good things in life. All that come from your formative years where you heard things that stuck.

We are all made up of these. Our own past experiences where we created beliefs, even as children.

E.g.

You might have done the best picture ever in school and wanted to show your mum, you were so excited to come out of school and show her and she is busy chatting to Mrs Jones. "Mum, mum", you shout "look at this". "Just a minute dear I am speaking". In that moment you create a belief that whatever you do is not good enough, even though she was just being polite. When you were that little child you created a load of beliefs that will not be serving the adult you. So it is time to question all beliefs and dismiss the ones that are holding you back.

Many beliefs were instilled in us as children by parents, teachers, siblings, and other authority figures. Up until the age of about 8, we cannot distinguish between fact and someone else's opinion, so much of what we were taught is accepted by our unconscious mind without question. We might have experienced things ourselves, or watched other people's lives unfold, and created limiting beliefs around that.

None of these beliefs were instilled in us with bad intent and it will serve you well to heal your blocks with the understanding that everyone is doing the best they could with what they had within them. After all, our parents and caregivers are made up of the limiting beliefs they adopted too. They just might not have cleared any of theirs.

As children, we may have been told that we were "stupid" or "clumsy" or "worthless" or would "never amount to much" or "rich people are all selfish, mean crooks" or "there is never enough" and those ideas often still govern our behaviour as adults. So we end up sabotaging our efforts at success.

All these things can hold us back from manifesting what we want.

The good news about beliefs is they can change. After all, I bet you believed in Father Christmas, Santa, the Tooth fairy and maybe even the Easter Bunny. Whilst as a little child you fully believed and now you don't. So that proves to you that you can change any belief with a bit of inner work.

Warning: I am going to give you some exercises to do to look at your beliefs. If you find there are very painful memories and experiences coming up, please seek appropriate professional help for you to deal with them.

Exercises:

Spend some time journaling on the following with the aim of identifying your beliefs. Think about what it was like growing up, what you were told was true, and what beliefs you have adopted and now believe.

1. Money Story

From as far back as you can remember, what did you hear or experience around money?

What is money for you?

2. Love Story

From as far back as you can remember, what did you hear or experience around love?

What is love for you?

3. Health Story

From as far back as you can remember, what did you hear or experience around health?
What is health for you?

Listen to your thoughts and your language that you use to describe them.

Clearing Your Money Blocks

If it is money that you really want to manifest please work through this section too. Money is actually a tool. It has no power, but you have the power to attract more of it to you.

If you believe you can only manifest money by your work, you are probably believing you have to work hard for your money. I would question that, because for a belief to be true it has to be 100% true. I know many people who do not work hard, but still have the money they need, me included. I know people who have won large lumps sums of money, been gifted money, found money. As long as you hold on to that belief that you have to work hard for your money, you always will.

If you have to work hard for your money, wouldn't all hardworking people be rich?

Yes, they would and that is not true so neither is that belief. So poke around at your beliefs and see what you are believing as true that is holding you back.

The truth is, I was not a stranger to money issues. I fought for too long trying to manifest money into my life until I stopped fighting and coming from a place of lack. I honestly believe the rich get richer and the poor get poorer because that is what they are focusing on.

My money story changed when I did exactly this. I was in such a stuck place, each day having to check accounts, you know the feeling of pinching from Peter to pay Paul, hoping there would be enough. I had anxiety about the future, until I got present to the now.

I got out my sticky financial situation by living for just today. Each day I asked myself, do I have enough money for today? If the answer was yes I said good, then all I have to do is enjoy myself. I took my focus off tomorrow and future money issues and on to today.

I focused on feeling as good as I could. I put music on whilst I went about my day. I made sure I laughed, did many things off my "Things To Do When Feeling Blue" list and because my energy shifted so did my financial situation, clients booked, money flowed and before long I had this huge sense of trust that everything always works out for me and it did.

You might consider yourself a born worrier and believe me I have met a lot. They worry about everything, themselves, other people, situations, the world they are in. I just want to really be clear here as it is an important message ***worrying is manifesting exactly what you don't want.***

Please don't tell me you can't stop, because you can if you believe you can. A further point is you didn't come into this world worrying, you don't see any babies worrying. It is a learnt behaviour. So it can be unlearnt too. I am not saying it is going to be easy to begin with but it will be hugely worthwhile.

If you are worrying about others, your partner, children, you are adding to their problems, creating more negative energy around them.

Instead, trust and believe they will find their way through whatever it is. That is honestly the best thing you can do for them.

If you are worrying about money right now, do you think that if you had all the money you want you would stop worrying about money? NO! You won't.

If you worry about not having enough money will it bring more money to you? NO! It won't.

The worrying about money is actually pushing it away from you right now.

So you have to do something else. It is a choice - you can always choose to feel better, choose to do something else.

Exercises – *For Money*

Here are some exercises regarding money you might like to try, and personally I love to do these, they are so much fun:

1. If money was a person exercise

Step 1: Write a letter to money as if you were having a relationship with it. It might come out something like this…..

Dear Money, Why are you never there for me? I can't rely on you. You seem to disappear as fast as you arrive. I want to spend more time with you, know you are really there for me. But I can't fully trust you. You come and go, I never know when you are going to turn up. You totally stress me out and cause me so many problems. X

Ask yourself, if you were money would you want to hang out with you? If you thought so badly of it, no probably not.

Step 2: Now write a letter of apology to money. Here is an example:

Dear Money, I am so sorry I have thought so badly of you. All these years I believed that you would never be there for me. I realize now it was my lack of trust and limiting beliefs creating this situation. I know you have done nothing wrong and I am looking forward to our new abundant relationship that will continue forward from now. X

Notice how much better that feels?

Step 3: Now write a love letter to money. For example:

Dear Money, Wow, I am adoring you being in my life. I love how you are so reliable, always there for me. You show up in the most surprising of ways and always delight me. I love how you always want to be around me and love having you in my life. Each day our relationship deepens and I fully trust you as you bring such ease and flow to my life. X

Now wouldn't that be a better relationship to have with money?

2. Account for all your money today – even if you have no money, you will be richer than you think. Today you need to account for every penny you have. Money down the sofa. The balance in old accounts. Gift vouchers you haven't used. Cash at the bottom of your bag or in the pocket in the car. Gather it all up and give gratitude for it. Notice how much more money was around you that you were not even acknowledging. We are always more abundant that we think and when you start being grateful for what you have money will flow to you.

3. Count up – count up all the money that comes to you in a week, or give what you receive a monitory value e.g. free cups of tea, discount vouchers, all income of all sorts, dinner at friends, gifts. Keep a record of it then give gratitude for it. Like above, start being grateful for what you have already and more will flow.

Common Blocks, Fears and Limiting Beliefs

Sometimes it is hard to identify a list of blocks, limiting beliefs and fears which may or may not affect you. It is not uncommon to know you have a block but to not know what it is or where it has come from. It may be deep inside you, even from a past life, it might be because it relates to a difficult situation.

I am including a list. By going through this list you will be able to easily say yes or no. The trick here is to use your unconscious mind not your conscious mind. That is the part of you that answers immediately and doesn't sit and think. It is a spilt second decision, just use your intuition.

Common Blocks – write in your journal which apply to you. It might be things you say, feel or actually honestly believe. Even if you are undecided about something write it down anyway as you can re-check it later.

Money Blocks

If it is more money you want, did you hear any of these when you were growing up?

- Money is hard to come by.
- There isn't enough money.
- You have to work hard for your money.
- Money doesn't come easily.

- You can't have time and money.
- We have always scrimped and saved for everything we have.
- Money is the root of all evil.
- Money doesn't buy happiness.
- Money doesn't grow on trees.
- I am from a poor, working class background.
- Money always seems to slip through my fingers.
- You have to rip people off to have money.
- Who did they rob to get that nice car/ house?
- The higher you go, the harder you fall.
- If I have money, that means other people will have less.
- I shouldn't be greedy.

Maybe you think:

- I never have money.
- Money stresses me out.
- I don't deserve a lot of money.
- Having money means you have to sacrifice your integrity.
- I don't like rich people.
- Rich people are snobs.
- I can't have money and love.
- I don't need a lot of money, just enough.
- Money isn't spiritual.

Are you always expecting:

- Things to always go wrong for you?
- There is never enough money to go round?
- That you can't afford it?

Health Blocks

- Are you using Google as a health checker?
- Are you always joining support groups for conditions?
- Are you always talking about your illnesses?
- Are you expecting the condition because it runs in the family?

Business Blocks – do you say?

- I am not good with money.
- I don't have a business head.
- I hate marketing.
- I can't do sales.
- I can't find the help I need.
- I'll just stick to what I am good at.
- I just want someone to tell me what to do.
- I am just not lucky.
- Nothing ever works.
- I can't work any harder.
- I'm too busy to try.

- I'm bad at networking.
- I don't know the right people.
- I am not good with technology.
- I am too old.
- I can't take risks.
- I hate my job but it pays the bills.
- It is too scary to try something new.
- My life is falling apart, I can't try something new.
- It's not the right time.
- There is never enough time.
- I am too busy.
- If I get it, I might lose it.

You should now have lots of possible blocks. I'm sure there are plenty more too so feel free to add to the list. Can you see how limiting your beliefs, can be?

Whilst this list of individual blocks above might seem a big problem to you they will be driven by something even bigger – a common limiting belief. In fact many blocks will have the same limiting belief behind it.

Beliefs are sneaky and can be hidden and dressed up as other things. They often don't present as not feeling worthy or deserving but instead you find yourself saying things like.

- I am too fat.
- I will never find the job I want.
- I'm not a lucky person.
- Others are better than me.
- I have too many responsibilities to create the life I want.
- I want….. but….

So ask yourself what is driving that block? Maybe a feeling of being not good enough, clever enough, pretty enough. Not deserving enough to have what you want.

- Here are some Common Limiting Beliefs – that you might identify with. They sit behind all the negative thoughts you are telling yourself and are often driving much smaller beliefs.
- Fear of not being Enough.
- Fear of Worthiness.
- Fear of not being Loved.
- Fear of Rejection.
- Fear of Failure.
- Fear of Success.
- Fear of Deservingness.
- Fear of being Judged.
- Fear of our Greatness.

Chapter 8

The Clearing Process

Hopefully you have now identified some blocks, fears and limiting beliefs and we are ready to clear them.

Step 1 – Is it true?

Knowledge is always power. Knowing you have got these blocks and limiting beliefs, means you can do something about them.

Quite honestly you are not the same person now as when you adopted or created a particular block or limiting belief and sometimes you can just cross it out and say, "no I don't believe that anymore", and it is gone.

For the blocks and limiting beliefs you have on your list ask yourself are they really true? For them to be true they have to be 100% true.

Can you think of examples where a block or limiting belief it is not true, maybe in the lives of others. If it can happen for others it can happen for you too.

The blocks and limiting beliefs you are left with, you can turn around with a positive affirmation.

Step 2 – Your desires

Journaling is good, better than just thinking, or saying things out loud I totally recommend talking to yourself. Fab on car journeys (on your own) or when you are home alone.

Ask yourself these 3 questions which I covered early in Creative Journaling:

1. **What do you want?**
2. **Why do you want it?**
3. **How will it feel?**

This is what we need to focus on, how will it feel? It is also the bit people often find tricky. Articulating the actual words to describe how it will feel is often tricky, but use a dictionary, thesaurus or good old Google if you need to.

Example:

- What do you want?
  E.g. Happiness, success, more money, holiday, new job etc
  Be specific on what exactly you want.

- Why do you want it?
  E.g. what will it give you? How will it change your life? What will you be able to have, or be able to do or experience by having it?

- How will it feel?
  This is really the important bit, it is the language the Universe speaks.
  When you have the thing you want, how will it feel?

Point to remember:

It rarely is the money we want, it is what we think the money will give us. This is where so many go wrong. Whilst we need to be clear about, the amount of cash we want coming in each month. Or for something specific and £1 is no different to £1000 to the Universe. However, a much more effective way of manifesting is to focus on what you want to do with the money rather than the money itself.

So how it feels driving that new car, or how that feels to live in the new home, not the money.

Let's be honest apart from the initial excitement the money might bring, it is very hard to visualise and access feelings on the money itself.

It is the same in business. It is not about the amount you earn but how it will feel doing the work. So focus on serving and the money becomes the by-product. Feel into working with your clients, the experience for the customer and then the effect the money will have in your life.

You can still focus on the actual figure you want to earn each month in your affirmations etc as the Universe likes clarity.

However it is much easier to focus on the things it will give you, not on the money.

Ok, great work, now you know what you want, why you want it and how it will feel. You should be crystal clear on that. Plus have an awareness of your blocks and limiting beliefs around what you want.

Step 3 – Now

How do you feel now?

The situation you are in **without** what you want?

Again be expansive and describe it, you might be feeling frustrated, sad, annoyed, disappointed.

This will highlight the gap between where you are in terms of your feelings and where you want to be, as in the feelings you will get when you have what you want.

Step 4 – The Gap

Now you are clear on what you want, think about your beliefs around what you want, including the ones you have identified earlier. Are they supporting the things you want to manifest?

If yes – great.

If not move on to step 5.

Step 5 – Reprogram Yourself For Successful Manifesting

To manifest successfully we need to believe it is possible. Great if your beliefs match your desires. If they do you should manifest in super-fast time, if not you will need to create some beliefs aligned to what you want. You can do these as Mantras or Affirmations to allow them to sink into your unconscious mind.

Now we need to believe we have it already. I call this FAKE IT TILL YOU MAKE IT. Or more accurately FEEL IT TILL YOU MAKE IT!

This isn't flippant but honestly what you need to do.

It is about changing your beliefs so ask yourself, "What beliefs about money would serve me better?"

Maybe something like "I am abundant, I am prosperous I am good at managing my money, money flows to me, I make good business decisions". Choose what fits best for you and start to repeat these phrases.

- At first this may seem very alien to you and you will probably hear a lot from the little "Gremlin voice" which tells you why that is not a truth for you. It is important to find ways to silence it. You might just want to tell it to do one and shut up! Really it works!

- Start to take actions to make those beliefs a reality. Maybe that is something as simple as keeping track of your spending or opening a savings account.

You could ask yourself "What beliefs would successful, prosperous people have about money", or "What beliefs would someone have that has what you want?"

- You will probably find that most of the beliefs held by successful, wealthy, prosperous people would be the complete opposite of what a person who was struggling with money would have.

- They look at what they can do, not what they can't do in life.

- They expect things to work out for them and if they don't they look at what they can learn from the experience and move on.

- There is a lot we can learn by looking at successful people.

Feel good about your money/health/love

When you think about the thing you want, what feelings do you get? Do you feel worried, panicky, sick in the pit of your stomach or that there is not enough?

Have you ever noticed that, when you worry about the lack of money, more things seem to go wrong, more unexpected bills come in and there seems to be a huge hole in your pocket? It seems the more you worry, the worse it gets.

So how do you turn that one around?

- Please remember that money is only a tool. It serves You. You don't serve it. It has no power, only the power you give to it. You hold the power.

- It is important to get into a good feeling place around money. Be grateful for what you have and what you can do with what you have right now. How much pleasure could you get out of what you have right now?

- Think of a time when you did something or you bought something where money (and it may not have been very much) gave you real joy or pleasure. Maybe it was a family outing or a meal with a friend or a holiday or something special you bought for yourself.

- The more you can remember those wonderful feelings about money and can call on them at will, the easier it is to attract things into your life that you want.

Step 6 – Affirmations Please see Chapter 5
Step 7 – Visualizations Please see Chapter 5
Step 8 - EFT – Tapping
So if your block hasn't cleared yet it is time again to crank it up a gear!

EFT is Emotional Freedom Technique or also called Tapping. I totally recommend you try this as it is a great way to break blocks down. I am not a practitioner but am sharing because I personally find it so useful. On YouTube you will find some great scripts to follow. I particularly love Brad Yates. Below I have included my own personal way of doing it, which combines it with journaling.

Preparation

- Allow the memories or emotions to come up and think about them, it is ok to be upset. Ask your Angel to support you.

- Journal on it - make notes about how you feel and ask yourself out loud why you feel like that.

- Write down all the negatives you feel.

- Grade how charged the emotion is from 1-10 (1 low 10 high) e.g. how upset/angry/scared you feel.

- Then ask yourself some questions - what is it you want? Why you want it? What is stopping you? The negatives you have written, are they true? Really try and rationalize your negative notes and get some positive statements.

- The next question to ask is what is the worst that could happen, this should highlight your fear. Again rationalize it, but whether it is really true, or has ever happened before.

- By the end of journaling you should be able to compile two lists. One of negatives and one of positives around what it is you want.

Set Up Statement

Create a statement that summarises your fear or issue. Then add on to the end of it, "I completely love and accept myself."

E.g. *Even though I'm scared.... I completely love and accept myself.*

Other examples:

- Even though I don't work hard enough...
- Even though it's extravagant to want more...
- Even though I have this guilt...
- Even though I don't like addressing this......
- Even though I am procrastinating.......
- Even though I'm greedy…
- Even though I am feeling selfish….
- Even though I am worried….
- Even though I don't know how this can happen…..

Tap three times on your karate chop point (side of your hand) repeating the sentence.

E.g. Even though I'm scared, I completely love and accept myself.

Negative Round

Use all the negative words and statements you journaled as you go round each of the tapping points with - I completely love and accept myself – on the end of each statement.

- Tap all Points:
    - Top of head,
    - Third eye,
    - Corner of eye near nose,
    - Outside of eye,
    - Under eye,
    - Lip,
    - Chin,
    - Collar bone,
    - Under arm on bra strap,
- Generally take 2 or 3 rounds of it and then you will feel the emotion lowering.
- Once your score is under 5/10 you can move on to positive round.

Positive Round

- Now repeat like the negative round but with positive statements and words you have journaled on, e.g. I have faced things like this before. It is getting easier to do this. I will not let this stop me.
- Again do 2 or 3 rounds until score comes down to 3 or under

With big issues you may need to do this daily for a few days and commit to a decent amount of time, so set a stop watch on your phone for 15 to 20 mins.

It is hard to explain this fully so I have created a video for you. You can watch a full demonstration of this on this link you will find in Chapter 14.

Step 9 - Release Work

Breath work is hugely beneficial for releasing trapped and stuck energy in your body. Here is a simple exercise you can try.

- You breathe in for the count of 5 thinking about the issue for example "I don't feel worthy". Or, "I am scared of trying". Or "Nothing is working out for me".

- Breathe out for the count of 10 saying RELEASE and squeeze it out of your body.

It is important for your out breath to be double the length of your in breath.

Whatever it is, keep trying everything until those blocks are gone. Trust me when I say they will keep popping up but now you have some tools to help you get through them, you will no longer be held back.

Chapter 9

Following Your Guidance

Inspired Action
Grounding & Protection
Meditation

Inspired Action

We need to remember we are not manifesting on our own but with the support of "The Upstairs". They will help us in so many ways and I go more into this in my first book – *Do I have an Angel?*

Listening to the guidance from "The Upstairs" is important, and so is acting upon it.

The real problem is how do we know when it is "them" or us just making it up?

Only by understanding your own energy will you get to know whether it is you or them.

When we are manifesting yes we need clarity on what we want. We need to align our energy to that which we desire. There is one final step, this is taking action. Not just any old action but inspired action. Action we feel drawn to take. It comes from deep within, the higher self, your intuition and of course the "The Upstairs" and it does not come from our heads.

You will be able to feel it, you will know it and honestly you can't doubt it. If you feel unsure that is not inspired guidance.

You might be looking to buy something and you feel inspired to look on a certain website or speak to someone who will tell you where you can find it.

It feels very natural and compelling. It feels right within you. It is interesting as so many manifesting practices tell you to visualize but they never tell you to take inspired action, I believe this is vital if you want to be a successful manifester.

Our Angels and Guides are often dropping guidance upon us, where do you think the lightbulb moments come from?

So the more you can understand yourself and be aware of your own energy the better, then you won't doubt the guidance you get.

Inspired guidance can come via meditation, quiet time, listening and often when you are doing something else. Driving for me is a great place that I get my inspired hits. Wherever you get yours, it is important to act upon it.

If you ask for guidance within meditation and feel you don't get anything back, don't worry. It might arrive with you later that day when you come across something and you know that is your answer.

Guidance isn't just heard, it is often felt and you translate it into words. Guidance can be a feeling, a sense, a knowingness. If it feels right and feels like a sign whether it is in meditation or just as you go about your day, it is a sign.

It is easy to miss signs when we are racing along going 100 miles per hour. That is why grounding and protection or better still meditation will help you understand your guidance.

Grounding and Protection

Grounding and Protection exercises are something I recommend you do every day to help you tune into you. We are all busy people, we are rushing around and don't take those important few minutes each day to be still and listen, to tune into ourselves and "The Upstairs" who are wanting to help us.

This is one of the reasons I am so passionate about Grounding and Protection. Not really to keep you safe but to keep you tuning into you. We don't really need a lot of protection when we have our Angels working with us, in fact often the biggest protection we need is protection from ourselves when we self-sabotage.

Either way, Grounding & Protection will help you tune into you. It will also protect you against negative energy that can drain you. We all have those people around us that we may well love but they just drain us. It is about being protected as much as possible with them but also knowing to limit your time with them too.

The grounding element literally keeps you grounded in the life you are in. After all we are spiritual beings having a human reality and it is important for us to be grounded so we can function. Floating through life away with the fairies is not practical.

Grounding and Protection can be as quick or as slow as you like. Some days I spend a few minutes doing this before a simple meditation. Other days I take my time. I also say to my clients that this is something never to skip, even if you are running late, do it sat on the loo, brushing your teeth or even in the shower. You will find your day goes a lot smoother if you do. The days I have missed doing it (which are very few) they have been extremely unproductive.

I am going to describe a really simple way to do this, but I do have **The Basics MP3** on my website that you can purchase to learn more or you can become a member of **Abundance Club** where we do this and a whole lot more. You will find links in Chapter 14.

Exercise – *Ground & Cleanse*

Visualize roots growing out of your feet, growing deep into the Earth, through all the different layers, splitting and branching as wide as they are going deep. Right down to the centre of the Earth where they tap into a beautiful bright white light. Allow your roots to drink up the light with every breath you breathe in. It comes up the roots into your body and fills up your body with the beautiful white cleansing light. When you are full of the white light, as you exhale and start to breath out the white light which cleanses your aura and leaves you grounded.

Exercise – *Protection*

Visualize putting on a cloak of protection. It can be any colour you like and it is super reflective. Do it after grounding and cleansing as you don't want to trap any negative energies under it. Let it wrap all around you and it has a hood that goes over your face. Know by having this cloak on you are bouncing back any negative, draining energies you come into contact with.

Do both of these daily. I often like to add a chat with my Angels on to the end of these each day too. You could ask a question that you want some guidance on and see what you get. Remember to trust and you will know in time whether it is you making it up or real guidance you need to act upon.

It only takes a few minutes and you can go as fast or slow as you like or times allows.

Meditation

Meditation is something I love to do and there are many ways to do it. It is often referred to as a meditation practice which means it needs practise.

No two meditations are ever the same. It is a bit like sex, sometimes you want it to last forever and it's amazing, another time if you have a lot on your mind you just want to get it over with and then you can get on with your day. You get the idea I'm sure.

There is nothing better than a meditation when you can't feel the difference between your nose and toes.

You feel total oneness and connection to source energy. I wish I could say it was like that every time but it is not. Sometimes you may fall asleep. Other times you can't switch the mind monkey off! So many fail because they suffer from the mind monkeys, the mind which keeps thinking. You can end up thinking of anything, replaying scenarios, thinking what should you have for tea, wondering if you remembered to lock the door. Yep, the head won't stop processing, so the benefits are lost because you can't get past that. Honestly, this happens to us all at some point but read on as there are ways past this.

I like to save full meditation for days when I have more time. I like to mix it up, sometimes I do guided, sometimes sound e.g. Ohm, sometimes just free meditation where I follow my breath. Please don't think meditation is the only way you can connect, it is just one way.

You will find some free meditations in Chapter 14.

Meditation is often over thought. People really wonder if they are doing it right, not sure what to expect. They try one type and if it doesn't go right, often think they can't meditate, so give up.

Meditation is a great way to get your guidance. It might be the step you need to take to make your manifestation turn up.

I want to reassure you that getting disturbed when you meditate is not dangerous. There is nothing to fear from meditation, only lots to gain.

Meditation is a way of quietening the busy mind, bringing in peace and enlightenment. It helps with stress and other medical conditions and of course is a great way to communicate with "The Upstairs" and get guidance on what action you need to take to make your manifestation turn up.

Different Types of Meditation

There are so many different types of meditation and it is important to find the right one for you:

- Focused-attention meditation, such as using a mantra or breath work.
- Mindfulness where you just allow thoughts to come and go.
- Buddhist Meditation.
- Sound Meditation like 'Om'ing.
- Transcendental Meditation (TM).
- Guided Meditations like I share in Abundance Club.
- Walking Meditation.
- Free meditations, just going within and connecting with "The Upstairs".
- Plus, much more, including activities like yoga etc.

So when you try one and it doesn't work for you, look at others as I am sure there will be one to suit you.

Simple Steps to Meditate

If you are struggling to meditate here is a simple process to get you started:

1. Set the intention – focus on what you want to achieve from the meditation session, maybe clear your head, relax or receive guidance.

2. Set a timer, 30 seconds for the first time and then build it up a minute or two at a time.

3. In that time just focus on your breath, count your breaths in and out.

4. Each time you lose focus just come back to the breath, as time goes on you will be able to increase the length you stay in meditation.

Meditative Exercises

Sometimes we don't need to do full meditation, as to get the benefits we can just do something really simple and still experience the results. Things like driving, exercising, sitting in the garden watching the birds and watching a fish tank can all be meditative, allowing your thoughts to flow and guidance to come in.

Tips to Help You Meditate

You need to find the right time of day for you, some like to meditate first thing, some prefer before bed, I personally like early morning after I am fully awake otherwise I go back to sleep.

It is really important to find the time that suits you, there is no right or wrong. I used to do mine after dropping my children at school and do it sat in my car in the driveway, as I knew if I went into the house I would get distracted and never find the time. I also used to do it differently at a weekend. I used to go and let the dog out and bring a cup of tea back to bed before anyone else woke and do it then. When the weather's nice there is nothing better than outdoors.

The only place you should not meditate is whilst driving or operating machinery for obvious reasons!

- To meditate you need to be in a quiet, comfortable place. At first, this might be in your home. Somewhere without interruptions (if possible)! Though when you become more advanced you can download these onto your device and play with headphones sat on a bench in your favourite place too!

- Don't lie down as you probably will go to sleep, but a blanket is useful to keep you warm. Think for a moment why often you see people sat crossed-legged meditating, you certainly couldn't go to sleep in that position. You could try a straight-backed chair too.

- Keep your arms unfolded to help the energy flow and take off restrictive and tight clothing.

- Try to ignore distractions and focus on you and this special time.

- Try to stay with it but don't worry if you drift off or start to think of something else. As soon as you are aware of this, just try and get back into it.

Meditating does take practice and you may not meet who you thought you would, or do what you think you should, but be assured you will get from it exactly what you need. Just give it another go next time.

Sometimes if you have gone into meditation to seek an answer and you come out and think you didn't get the answer, don't think you did something wrong. It might be that later in the day you come across your answer by seeing or hearing something.

Document Your Meditations

You might like to keep pen and paper to hand when meditating, ideally your journal. Then you can jot down what you experience in your meditation as lots of golden nuggets of insight can come through in them.

I am sure you will end up loving meditation as much as I do. I do some type of meditation every day and the more I meditate the more I feel connected to "The Upstairs".

Chapter 10

Stopping Self-Sabotage

We all trip ourselves up from time to time and self-sabotage our success in manifesting. In this chapter we are looking a bit more at what you might need to address if this is happening for you.

Upper Limits

Sometimes our manifesting is going so well and life feels amazing, then bump it stops. We think about what have we done and we really don't know what the problem is. We could manifest the things we wanted last time but now it feels like we are stuck again. We can't get past that upper limit.

As we work towards our goals and intentions, it is very common for us to find we sabotage ourselves.

- We might start to better our health, and then binge on junk food.

- We might decide to get fit, feel on track for a while and then find ourselves drinking wine at night rather than going out for a walk or run.

- We might get our business going well and then get ill.

- We might get a new relationship and then pick an argument.

- We might even find that when really big and exciting things do happen, another area of our lives seems to fall apart.

Why does this happen? According to Gay Hendricks, author of *The Big Leap,* we each have an internal thermostat that determines how much love, abundance and success we believe we are worthy of, or that is our norm.

When we go above that, we will "Upper Limit" ourselves. This is the term he uses to mean we've hit our ceiling. We might fear that this positive phase can't last, sabotage ourselves in some way, or we don't allow ourselves to enjoy our successes.

The first step is to notice it then address it with The Clearing Process in Chapter 8. Just treat it like another block and follow the process and you will get through it.

Self-Worth

There are so many aspects to worthiness. It is the biggest core block, the one that is driving others.

- You may feel worthy of money, but not the abundance of money you really want. So you always only just have enough.

- You may feel worthy of love but not the loving relationship you really want.

- You may feel worthy of health but not the full health you actually want to experience every day.

- You may feel worthy of success but not to the level you really dream of.

Can you see how there can be different levels of worthiness?

People with low self-worth often don't live their true manifesting potential. They may allow others to not treat them how they really want as they don't honestly feel worthy of it. This will block manifesting and leave them with a low vibe energy.

Alternatively, if you have high self-worth you don't stop reaching for what you want. You don't let anyone stand in your way.

Tips for increasing your self-worth:

1. At the end of each day write down 3 things you feel proud of about yourself from that day, it might only be that you held your tongue. Or took some time for you.

2. Tell someone else how much you appreciate them, remember the Universe is like a mirror so it will reflect back to you what you give it.

3. Set some boundaries. Ask your Angels to help you say no! They will help you say no from a place of love without offending the person asking you for some help.

4. Everything you do, do it to the best of your ability, develop a reputation as someone who takes pride in their work.

5. Walk tall and proud remembering, even better repeating, a positive affirmation.

6. Dress smart so you feel good.

7. Do something for yourself every day.

8. Learn a new skill or take up something you've always wanted to and stick with it.

9. Speak up for yourself in every area of your life. This might be hard to do at first but the first time you do it will be immense and if you carry on your self-worth will soar. Ask your Angels to help you.

10. When the negative mind monkeys creep in just tell them to do one, and disappear. You haven't got time for them. You have an awesome life to build.

You could also go over this in The Clearing Process in Chapter 8.

Boost Yourself

Your Angel already thinks you are amazing, isn't it time for you to believe it too? I am going to give you an exercise to do that will probably make you squirm. In fact, if it does that will be a sure sign you have low self-esteem or self-confidence, but don't worry as we can fix it.

Exercise –*To Feel Good About Yourself*

You will need your journal and you are going to write a different header at the top of three different pages.

Headed up as follows:

1. Things I am good at:

2. Things I have achieved:

3. Things I like about myself:

Start by adding as much as you can under each header from the little stuff to the big, from the stuff when you were at school to now. Everything! Go as far back as you can remember.

When you are done, put it to one side and the next day add some more to it.

When you are totally sure there is nothing else you can add ask your nearest and dearest to add to it.

You might find some things go under more than one header and honestly is doesn't matter which one you put them under, just make sure you don't list things more than once.

When you have got it complete, read it back to yourself and ask yourself this….

If I met someone like that who had all of those incredible qualities, what would I think?

You probably will think what an amazing person they are. That amazing person is YOU.

Refer back to the lists often, keep them to hand, in fact try reading them daily. Take a picture of them and put them as your wallpaper on your phone or computer. When you see it all on paper you will realize how amazing you actually are.

Self-Love

Self-love is important for everyone, whatever you want to manifest, but especially if you want to manifest a love relationship. After all, how can you expect someone else to love you when you don't love yourself.

Notice when you look in the mirror, do you cringe, put yourself down or do you give yourself a bit of self-love and say something nice?

When you look in the mirror it is a great time to give yourself some love and positive vibes, whatever the reflection is bringing up for you.

Say I love you. You look great. Thank you. Well done. Anything you like, but don't put yourself down.

How can you go out and manifest magic if you are putting yourself down? It doesn't help at all and needs to stop.

If you do catch yourself saying anything negative fix it by saying 3 positive things. You will soon start to turn it around.

I was staying in a hotel with my daughter as we were attending an event. In the morning when we were ready I stood in front of the mirror and said out loud. "You look great, have a fantastic day".

My daughter said, "You didn't just say that to yourself did you?"

"Of course I did", I told her. If I can't say it who else is going to.

Can you imagine the difference in my energy as I started my day and entered a room full of women. If I had said to myself, "You look fat, that really doesn't suit you. Why did you pick that outfit?" Remember everything starts inside out.

Notice too when you get a compliment and someone says something nice to you. Do you accept it graciously or do you make an excuse and say, "Oh this old thing!"? Remember, with manifesting we always need to be able to receive, and this includes compliments.

Start to feel better about yourself now. What can you do to make you feel better today? These are my favourites.

- Sleep in your best bedding or PJ's.
- Burn your best candles.
- Always wear perfume.
- Have makeup on.
- Wear your best clothes when you are just staying in.
- Put some lip-gloss on.
- Wear your best underwear.

I am sure you get the idea; it is all about feeling good about yourself. With manifesting it is always about feeling good. I never save things for best anymore, I like to live in the now.

Upgrades & Rewards

One of the things I like to do is upgrade my life a bit at a time and reward myself often. I have got to the point now where I can reward anything. Something I have achieved, something I have let go of, something I took action on. It matters not, I am all about rewards and giving myself acknowledgement. I am not waiting for an external source to acknowledge it, I do that for myself.

I often use upgrades as rewards as they make me feel good and I am sure by now you will have got the message that it is all about how you feel.

It is a fun activity to go around your home and life and think about what you want to upgrade. You are probably very aware of all the big things you want, but what about the little things.

You can even put them all on a vision board if you wish (see Chapter 12).

Take a look at your home and life and see what you wish to upgrade, think of all areas. Walk around your home and identify what could do with an upgrade. Make a list of things that will make you feel good.

- Underwear.
- Towels or tea towels.
- Clothes.
- PJ's.

- Skin care.
- Crockery.
- Bedding.

Then when you want to reward yourself for whatever reason, you can pick something from your list and upgrade. Or when your self-worth increases you may find that you don't even need to wait to reward yourself, you may do it anyway, which is even better because you feel worth it.

Chapter 11

Trouble Shooting

Manifesting Malfunctions
Dealing With Negative People
Staying High Vibe for Manifesting
Monthly Planning

Manifesting Malfunctions

Believe me, in the dance with the Universe you will have these from time to time. I still do. Maybe you have tried too hard and not trusted enough.

Sometimes, when we don't focus our energy in the right way, or overlook some detail, we don't manifest exactly what we want. Or maybe we think we have followed all the steps but our order did not arrive.

This is when I ask you to look carefully over what happened, did a little bit of doubt creep in?

Did you discuss it with someone else, which is fine, but maybe their response triggered something in you?

Really look back over the whole process, pull it apart and see what happened.

Don't feel upset, as that will bring more of that in. Instead learn from it and feel confident you know what went wrong and next time you will do it right. The Universe always delivers, so make sure you put your order in correctly!

So as we are drawing to an end. I am really hoping you have turned yourself into an incredible manifesting machine.

We have been aiming to get you into the manifesting zone, this is when the magic happens quickly. You literally just think about something and it happens. Powerful stuff, all supported by your Angels/The Upstairs/Source, tapping into Universal energy and resources, making life easier for yourself.

You become unconcerned about what you have no control over and the things you are not wanting. All your energy is working towards what you do want. So you are doing the things that make you happy and receiving more abundance.

This will mean you have more to give to others and you will be a happier person to be around.

However, let's also be realistic as there will be times when life can take over and sometimes we don't get round to doing our manifesting practice for one reason or another. We end up having a manifesting malfunction. So before we part ways let's cover what we do when this happens, because it will. It happens to us all from time to time.

The main thing is you don't let it knock you. You don't feel too bad, well not for long anyway. You have all the tools in here to get back on track, so don't beat yourself up about it. Remember ,how you feel is the most important thing, so the longer you feel bad about it the more rubbish you will be attracting to you.

Pick yourself up, brush yourself down and get back on that manifesting wagon.

Lift your chin up, put a smile on your face and get your groovy tunes on, dance yourself back into the manifesting zone, or whatever else you do to get into your happy space.

It might be that it just didn't happen at all or things go well for a while then you fall off your wagon and get out of the zone. Don't feel bad, it happens to us all, me included ,from time to time! There is one thing wrong when manifesting doesn't work and that is our energy is misaligned, so no biggy, we can soon realign ourselves again.

Now don't get me wrong it feels horrid, when this happens. You will find it hard to believe you could have done something wrong. You will be annoyed, cross and upset. You will want to give up and you might even be in panic mode.

This is when you need to look back to what threw you off. A slight comment from someone else, did your priorities change? Did you really commit to your daily practice every day?

You need to do one thing - **start again**! Not by being annoyed and upset with yourself and feeling like you have failed, but knowing you are learning and just because you didn't get it right that time doesn't mean you won't get it right next time.

You are wiser now, more in control to clear those blocks.

Remember – knowledge is power over those pesky blocks!

Go back to the start and use everything I have covered in here.

Maybe you need to look at your affirmations and see if they feel too far off. You might be saying "I am a money magnet", and all you feel is broke, so as you say it the mind monkey are saying, "Who are you kidding, have you seen the bills you have coming in?"

Yep, we have all been there. A nice way to bridge the gap, when where we are now and where we want to be seem too far apart, and it seems impossible, is the following:

Start by saying things are turning round and starting to get better. Start remembering your past successes not failings. Saying things like, "I am becoming better with money". "Each day I am becoming healthier". I am sure you get the idea.

Using the words **becoming and beginning** make it closer than you think. One day you will find you can say the statement comfortably and you will realize that you are actually becoming closer to your dreams. Great to use in your affirmations too!

e.g. Each day I am becoming wealthier or healthier or lighter.

It is good to use sayings like "I used to do that", or "I used to be like that", or "I used to have that".

e.g. I used to be bad with money…now I am good.

Try a different type of visualization. If you are a 'Future Diary' fan then give the 'Dear Universe' a go. Switch it up, see what a difference it can make. When we become complacent with our daily practice we can go through the motions of doing it without really feeling it.

Dealing with Negative People

I have included a bit about this as I hear so many of my clients saying how this is so difficult for them. Especially if they have a loved one that is negative. Sadly we can't manifest for anyone else. We can send the good vibes and trust they will get what they want.

However, if you are struggling with negative people around you the best thing you can do is be as positive as possible and they will eventually start to notice. You may find they want to know what you are doing and your positivity will rub off on them.

1. Do extra protection. Imagine mirrors all around you facing out reflecting back their negativity. Ask the Angels to strengthen your protection too.

2. Ask yourself why you are letting their negativity bother you? It's a great question to journal on.

3. Check it is not a projection of your own limiting and negative beliefs.

4. Try to understand what is going on for them and why they are negative about what you are being positive about. Do they have a fear attached?

5. Lead by example, be that person you want them to be.

6. Accept them as they are. Don't expect them to change, you have to be the change.

7. Don't label others as negative as you get what you focus on. If you expect them to be negative that is all you will see. People will only show the side of themselves that you expect.

8. No one has the power to make you feel anything that isn't already inside of you. If they have pushed your button, that button was already there. Do some inner work on yourself and be empowered. Thank them for showing you where you need to still do some work on yourself.

Another little exercise that is simple and has saved some of my client's marriages is this.

Exercise:

Write down the name of the person who is negative and you are struggling with. Write down 5 things you love, appreciate and like about them, then come up with 5 more and continue until the end of page. Go on for as long as you can if you can do more than one page, even better.

The next stage of the exercise is to remember what you loved and appreciated about them when you first met. So often in long term relationships we forget what we fell in love over and now just focus on the irritations. When you start to remember all those old things you loved and focus on the positives about them you start to see them in a different light.

Staying High Vibe for Manifesting

- Don't take offence, it weakens you.

- It's not about being right or wrong it is about being kind.

- Don't force and try too hard, as this comes from fear that you won't receive.

- Remember your job is not the HOW!

- Ask your Angels to make your heart and head to be in tune and asking for the same things.

- Don't ask repeatedly because you are worried or scared. Use that energy to relax and expect and believe you will receive.

- Make sure you are honest about what you want.

- Watch out for synchronicities as these are often big signs when manifesting.

- Don't worry, as that is manifesting something you don't want.

- Even if you don't exactly know what you want, by feeling a bit better each day, it will bring better things in.

- If you become unstuck use these affirmations: - Everything always works out for me. The Universe has my back. How can it get any better than this?

- Spend your time wisely and hang out with others that get this.

- The past is not important, so keep looking forward but really focus on now.

- Enjoy now and make peace with now, it is all we have.

- Book of Gratitude - add to it daily and refer to it often.

- Train yourself to have more positive thoughts. Set alarm reminders so you can remember to tune into yourself regularly and see how you are feeling. If you are feeling negative you flip your funk.

- Choose carefully who you spend time with you are the average of the 5 people you spend the most time with.

- Beware how negative social media can be and limit your time on it.

- When you fall off your manifesting wagon. Get back on fast!

- Keep in the flow, get and keep your practice going.

- Remember that different blocks will go at different points.

- Stay positive - give up the news.

- Challenge your beliefs, they are just stories you are telling yourself.

- Acknowledge good points. Praise yourself for how well you are doing, even reward yourself.

- Do things that make you happy.

- Get a mentor or a coach.

Monthly Planning

I recommend you tweak your manifesting practice each month. Create new affirmations and do a new type of visualization. Ideally because what you wanted has manifested.

If after a month of consistent practice what you have tried to manifest has not arrived address your blocks, fears and limiting beliefs as we have covered.

Remember not to try and manifest everything in one go, keep your energy focused on the one main thing you want and manifest in order of priority. I wouldn't do any more that 3 specific areas of your life in one go as it spreads your energy too thin.

Chapter 12

Other Ways To Manifest

Create Your Own Luck
Full Moon Manifestation
Vision Boards

Create Your Own Luck

Everything is about your beliefs, if you believe something will work it will. If you believe something is lucky it will be. I know myself that if I wear a certain pair of knickers that I consider to be my lucky knickers I will have a great day. You might have a lucky coin, crystal or something. It is only lucky because you believe it to be lucky, we always create our own luck!

Full Moon Manifestation

Manifestation is especially powerful when done with the full moon. Write down what you require or want. Put it in the light of the full moon on a window sill (either inside or out) with a quartz crystal for three nights, the night before the full moon, the night of the full moon and the night after. After the three nights burn the letter safely. Then wait for your special delivery! Just like all manifesting it is about your beliefs.

Vision Boards

Vision boards can also be called dream boards. There is something quite magical about them. I love how things just turn up for real, without any effort. It always surprises me when I come to re-do mine how many things have manifested without me even realizing.

What I really love about vision boards is you can put lots of different things on them, so you can think about all areas of your life. You can put pictures, photos, words, lists, images, anything you want.

It is so different from doing a daily practice, where you need to focus on the main things you want.

The **preparation of a vision board is very important** and **also the creating** of it.

If it feels like something you just need to get done, don't do it! Wait until it feels right and a good time. As everything is energy, the energy you are using when you make your board is important to how things will turn up.

Don't rush the preparation step, allow yourself to feel into everything you want to bring into your life. It is such a fun thing to do.

STEP ONE - Preparation of the board

Spend some time gathering images and other things you want on your board. You can cut things from magazines, print off images from the internet or even do one online.

I like to gather things for a while, creating a pile or a list of things I want to put on my board, giving some real thought to it, then go online and search the images in one go.

You can also have different boards for different areas of your life, if you wish. So for love life you might want a heart-shaped board. Or you can have one big board with everything on it.

You might want to think of words you want on it to describe the feelings you want to experience, like loved, respected, successful, rich.

On it you can put ribbons, stickers, even a £50 note if you want (my personal favourite).

There are no rules - it is what feels right to you.

STEP 2 - Creating the board

This is the most important time, so make it special. Put music on, light a candle, enjoy creating it. After all, you are building your life. It is such a fun creative way of putting it out there.

Make it from anything: paper, cardboard, picture frame or clip frame.

Even digitally: Pinterest, on a computer, or an app.

Pack it out with emotions, feelings, words, pictures. It is all about how you want to feel. **Feelings are the important bit!**

You can add to it when you want to.

I like to put a photo of me in the middle and then all my images and words around it. I keep each section for a different area of my life, but like I say, there are no rules.

I also use a clip frame and some sticky tac on my images so I can change them easily.

You can make vision boards with your partner too if you want the same things. Or get the whole family involved if it is something specific you all want, like a holiday.

If you are wanting to sell your house put an image on the board of the house with a sold sign, then a removal van, an image of the sort of place you want to move to.

If you have a business put on the amount of money you want to earn, or if you want a new job put the salary on you want.

STEP 3 – Using the vision board

Where to put your board

You could use Feng Shui to decide the best place for your board. So for example the south west corner is good for love. If you don't follow Feng Shui, don't panic it will still work.

It is all about your beliefs and believing in your board will make things happen for you. I would put your board somewhere you can see it often. The danger is it becomes part of the furniture and you never look at it.

It is good to visualize in front of it. Really look at everything every day and think how it will feel to have all that. I like to do that before I start work as I have mine in my office.

You can take a picture of it and use it as your wallpaper on your phone or computer.

How to make the vision board work faster

The more you visualize the faster it will all happen.

You need to align your energy to what you want and totally believe it is coming. You could do this by using affirmations relating to it.

What people often miss off their board

Vision boards are often just images, but it is the feelings that are important as they are what the Universe is listening to and more importantly delivering against. So make sure you have feelings on your board, either with words or images that portray that feeling to you, and make sure you look at your board often.

How vision boards can go wrong

- You don't give any time to it.

- You create it with the wrong energy.

- You don't look at it.

- You are not aligned to what is on it.

The most important thing is to believe and look at it often. Not fully believing it can manifest is often the biggest issues.

When to change you board

Change it regularly as things manifest. You can just take one thing off at a time if you use sticky tac like me, or change the entire board monthly, or every 6 months, it is up to you.

Here is a picture of one of my boards

Chapter 13

Inspirational True Manifesting Stories

In this chapter you will find inspirational manifesting stories of mine and my clients. Have a read of them when you feel you need a burst of inspiration because anything is possible as long as you believe.

I have manifested so many incredible things using a vision board. Here are some them:

Manifesting A Free Cruise

By Amanda Tooke

Cruises are my favourite type of holiday and I have done a few but it blew my mind when I manifested a free one!

We were in the middle of a house move and my trusty vision board that had lots of things on it including a cruise liner, fell apart in the move. It lived for a couple of weeks propped up, with the nose of the ship sticking up next to my desk, as if to remind me about a cruise.

It is exhausting moving house and I told my children that when we got settled I would sort out a holiday for us. "They asked what type it would be". "A cruise", I said looking at the ship popping up from the side of my desk.

Honestly I'm not sure they believed me, but I knew as I said it I was determined. A holiday was definitely what we needed. I was still quite open about where and when. Though I did think I didn't want it to be too hot so Spring would be nice time of year, it was February at the time.

Ten days into my move my phone binged and a text appeared:

Hi Amanda, I don't suppose u fancy a free 12nt cruise end of March….

It was one of those moments when you stare at your phone and wonder if you have read it correctly. A free cruise, surely not?

The thing is the Universe is always listening and always responding. It would have been easy to let my pride take over and say "No I can't", but that would not have been working with the Law of Attraction. Of course I had to say "YES PLEASE", and find out more.

It turned out to be from one of my VIP clients, a place had come available as one of her party couldn't go and she had offered it to me.

I was not going to turn down this. I had asked and the Universe had delivered. I was not specific in the details, but never in a million years did I think it would have been free. I have manifested many things in my time but never a free cruise. It still makes me smile how it all happened.

When the booking was transferred into my name it turned out it was a 4 berth cabin so I paid for my children to come along too.

Two Weeks To Manifest A New Car

By Amanda Tooke

We all have dreams, goals and aspirations. The thing that stops them from turning up is our beliefs. We block ourselves because often we don't think it will happen. We can't see how it is possible. It might seem too big of a thing. We are all born manifesters and often we are doing it unconsciously so we can manifest things we don't want.

You can't only buy into the Law of Attraction if it works. The Universe doesn't get it wrong, it is us that does. You can manifest anything physical things or emotional things. It comes down to you and what you want.

The thing is, as people, we like to be in control of the how and that is never our job. The Universe will deliver you your dreams if you believe in it and leave it to deliver them how it sees best.

So when I was wanting to manifest a new car it was very easy for me to get stuck in the how and think of all the ways I could make this possible.

Thankfully I didn't and here is how I manifested my dream car in just over 2 weeks. Of course you can use these tips to manifest whatever you want, it is down to you.

I made a decision on what car I wanted. This involved test driving cars to see what was right for me. I had leaflets and pictures which I placed on my vision board. I started to notice more and more of these cars everywhere I went, they were coming into my reality even if they weren't actually mine.

Once I was really clear on the make, model and colour combination, I kept thinking about it. Remembering how it felt when I was test driving it. However, I was grateful for the car I had and gave gratitude for it being reliable and getting me around.

I didn't repeatedly ask the Universe, instead I trusted that it would happen, but did not focus on the how. That is the job of the Universe. Instead I kept imagining how it would feel to drive it and to arrive wherever I was going in it. I could picture it on my drive too.

I imagined washing it, well taking it to the car wash! Visualized what my friends and family would say and the pleasure it would give me and the sense of achievement I'd feel by manifesting it. Every time some doubt came in I visualized harder and affirmed it would be mine.

It wasn't long before my old car needed to go in for a service. It has been in plenty of times before and I have always had the same sort of car, or something less in value, to use whilst it has been in.

I couldn't believe my eyes when I arrived that morning and my loan car was my dream car! It was exactly the make, model and even colour combination I had decided on and was in fact the car I test drove at the start. Blue with a sliver roof!

For whatever reason the garage were short of loan cars and used the demonstrator, little did they know it that was my dream car and the Universe was working its magic.

Well, I was very grateful I was self-employed and I made the maximum use of this car for the day, taking a day out with the family. I loved it and so did they. I even got my magnetic signs advertising my business off my old car and put them on it!

I took pictures of us in it and around it and parked it on my drive. I used these as wallpapers on my phone and computer, plus as more images on my vision board.

Sadly, this day came to an end and I really didn't want to take it back. However, I didn't let my mood dip, I was confident that it would be mine before long.

When I returned it I asked how much it would cost to get me into that model and colour combination. When the salesman tried to find out there were none available and offered to sell me that exact one at a reduced price!

I went home even more excited, feeling it coming even closer, but still giving gratitude for my car I was in. I gave it out to the Universe to send me the money required to take the leap up to the new car. I so wanted my Range Rover Evoque. I really didn't know how that would happen, maybe some windfall? I also knew not to get into the how but to trust instead.

People kept asking me questions, it felt like they were testing me, doubting it would happen, who can blame them as it was a big upgrade? Each time I took myself back to how driving it felt and trusted it would be mine soon.

As our job in manifesting is never the how, I had confidence in the Universe that it would happen and it did.

What actually happened is I was guided to offer my one-to-one programmes and all the places sold out without me even having a webpage advertising them.

I was inundated by clients asking me how I could help them more, so when I mentioned my new one-to-one programmes most said yes.

I couldn't believe it. Once I could see the flow of cash coming in I was on the phone to the garage placing my order as I didn't want anyone else getting my dream car.

This was a huge achievement for me, I can't tell you how buzzing I was when I picked the car up. The smell of the new car? And it was all mine. It too 2 weeks to manifest a new car!

Not bad for a single mum who launched an alternative business in a recession and hasn't looked back. My gorgeous car still makes me feel so abundant when I drive it.

So whatever your dreams are believe they are possible. Don't hold yourself back by getting stuck in the how. Miracles happen every day when you look for them. If I can manifest a new car in only 2 weeks to just think what you could do?

How I manifested my hot tub

By Amanda Tooke

I am a great believer in Vision Boards and tell all my clients to do them. I always have one on the go filled with big dreams and little things too. I love how things on them just turn up with very little effort. They really do make your dreams come true.

I have had something on my vision board for a few years now but have never been able to have it due to where we lived.

However, when we moved the new house had the perfect space for my own hot tub - one of my dreams.

I love water and often joke that I must have been a mermaid in a past life. I swim a few times a week and then sit in the hot tub and meditate at the leisure club. It is where I receive a lot of my guidance.

So when we moved house my dream of a hot tub felt closer than ever, so I cranked up my manifesting practices as I know when I do that it happens for real in no time at all.

I am a stickler for my manifesting practices. I have created a series of simple exercises to hold your energy in place so your manifestations turn up fast and in the most unexpected ways I teach these exercises in Abundance Club.

I started announcing to people that I was going to get a hot tub. I told clients, mentioned it in my free classes and spoke about it with confidence as I knew it would turn up when I did that.

When I put my furniture on the patio I left space for my hot tub. I have to say people did ask why there was a gap but I confidently told them that it was where the hot tub was going. It was funny to watch their raised eyebrows, but I had to leave space for it, so the Universe knew.

One day my son put some wood there and I asked him to move it as that was where my hot tub was going. He said, "You haven't even ordered it yet Mum". I told him it didn't matter, the Universe was dealing with it.

Even when we had my son's 18th birthday BBQ and chairs were placed where the hot tub was going I asked people if they were enjoying sitting in my hot tub. Some played along and some probably thought I was a bit mad, but I didn't care, I knew it was coming.

If others heard my family's conversations they would have thought we were bonkers. We said things like – don't go in the hot tub with your clothes on, careful you don't drip everywhere, I have had a tough day, can't wait to get in the hot tub, it's so lovely and warm in here, are you coming in?

I am sure you get the picture. I don't think there was anyone who didn't know I was getting one and it was great to have a family that would play along with it as they know how the Universe works.

When I was at the leisure club sat in their hot tub I would visualize being sat in mine on my patio.

It didn't take long and hot tubs kept coming into my reality everywhere I looked. On Facebook they were always coming up in my newsfeed.

I even went to the hairdressers one day and on the way there I came across a hot tub shop that I didn't even know was there before then. I said to the Universe that if there was a parking space I would go in, and sure enough there was. So I parked and went in.

I was looking at them all and knew what I wanted as I had tried many out over the years and I wanted one that would give really good massages. This was not a cheap purchase and definitely of a luxury indulgence, but I knew too I deserved it.

The cars, house, holidays all felt a necessary but the hot tub was certainly not an everyday item.

As I was talking to the man in the shop I felt the need to tell him I was manifesting a hot tub, about my vision board. He said, "Are you into all 'that' sort of stuff!" I said, "Yes I most certainly am, why?" He then asked me if I believed in Angels. Well, I guess you know the answer to that one.

We had a fab conversation about how he met his Angel when he had a near death experience. I took this as another sign.

I was still not sure how the hot tub would come or even the exact model I wanted but I knew it was closer than ever. When I got home I searched on the internet to find this hot tub shop I had been to and came across another a bit further away.

I decided to go and visit it the following weekend as it did preloved hot tubs. I was not keen on that idea to begin with but 3 people said to me, "Why don't you just get a used one?" so this synchronistic message hit home and I took it as a sign and something I should consider.

Later in the week, in the local supermarket, I found some plastic wine glasses that I thought would be perfect to have my Prosecco in sat in my hot tub, so I bought them confident I would be able to use them soon. This did get a snigger from a certain family member that thought I had done it the wrong way round. However, I had to show the Universe I was serious so it would deliver.

When I arrived at the showroom I was greeted by a lovely lady who explained everything and showed me round. She asked what I did and when I told her she lit up as she explained about how a little robin visits her in the office and she feels it is her dad.

Later on when we were sat down going through everything my voice went all croaky as it does when I have Spirit and I knew it was her dad. I couldn't carry on talking to her till I had delivered her message. She loved hearing from her dad and I knew this was the place to get my hot tub as I saw two tubs that were a perfect match for me.

One I could afford with ease, the other was a bit more pricey but newer and a better model making it cheaper to run. I went home with all the details to mull it over. I knew what I wanted but I also knew what I could afford.

After thinking about it, measuring it out, umming and ahing over it all, I made the sensible decision to go for the one I could easily afford. Though I have to say, even after I had made the payment I kept thinking, that I should get the other one.

So it came as no surprise when the day before I was meant to get the hot tub the man called me and said he had found a problem with the one I picked, it had developed a leak. Needless to say he offered me the one I really wanted instead at the same price. Why? Because everything always works out for me. It is my default setting with Universe.

MAKING DREAMS COME TRUE

My Dream Home

By Amanda Tooke

I have manifested many houses but my favourite one is the one I won ITV's *May The Best House Win* in.

We were living in a rented cottage and the lease was due to expire. We had 3 weeks left! I had thought I had found my perfect home and it all fell through, I was so disappointed. It would have been easy to think manifesting does not work. Instead I chose to believe something better would come along.

Within 24 hours 3 people had asked if I had I seen the house near the golf course.

I had seen it for sure, it had been empty for over 6 months. It was an amazing property, one dreams are made of, but I also knew it was double what I could afford.

Nevertheless I couldn't ignore the sign of 3 people mentioning it in 1 day. I went to view and couldn't believe it, it was more stunning in real life.

There were so many little white feathers I was sure I would find a dead bird, but I didn't.

I walked through the door and felt like I had come home.

The house was massive and had an annex which I was allowed to rent it out. That made it affordable.

Less than 2 weeks later we moved in, to a dream house that was double what I could afford.

You see the Universe is always listening, always delivering, I could have totally missed that opportunity if I had just thought of how I could afford it.

I lived there over 5 years and loved it.

Money From Nowhere

Anonymous

One of my favourite stories to share is how a client manifested money from nowhere!

She was a young single mum with two small boys and lived in a rural area. She relied on her car for getting the boys to school and usual family life.

Sadly the car was needing repairs and she didn't have the money. She also knew she couldn't survive living so rural without one.

She made the decision to send it to the garage anyway and trusted that the Universe would provide.

Whilst the car was in the garage she went to a Jumble Sale and picked up a book that she bought. When she got home and opened the book there was some Euros in it.

She is an honest lady so took it back to the Jumble Sale. No one knew where it had come from. So she was told to keep it.

When we converted the Euros to GBP it was exactly the amount she needed for the car repairs.

I still get goosebumps every time I share this magical story.

Manifesting A New Relationship

By Christina Butler

My manifesting story literally changed my life. I was a 63 year old lady who had been divorced after a 36 year challenging marriage. I felt it was time for me, but The Universe had other plans! After doing some work on myself, restoring my love for myself and others, I decided to give manifesting a new man into my life a go. I wrote down the type of man I was looking for, every detail and got really clear.

I starting my daily practice and guess what? He showed up and I have to say he loves me with such unconditional love. He allows me to be me, so no hiding anymore trying to be someone I am not. I got married last year. I had in the past manifested smaller things but this was the biggest one and the best. Go on, give it a go!

A New Car and Dream Job

By Simon Clarke

I wanted a new car and I pictured myself driving something that made me feel good driving it and proud to own it. That's when I spotted this green BMW 7 series. These cars are huge, and have massive engines. However, the fuel economy didn't matter as I lived only a mile away from where I worked, and walked in most days. I have to admit to having a bit of a geek crush on this car, not only did it have a car phone but it had a TV as well.

The interesting thing was that as I looked at it every week the price got lower and lower. When I finally went to look at it, drive it, and fall in love with it, the price had dropped even more and I was really happy to buy it at that price.

As soon as this car arrived I advertised my old car and the guy offered me the advertised price. I think there was literally a couple of hundred pounds difference between the prices of the two cars.

While that is a good example of the Law of Attraction working for me, let's get to the big one.

After working for the RAF for many years I found I was not going to be employed there much longer. Rather than trying to find a similar job to apply for I decided to use the Law of Attraction again, as it had worked for me last time.

With over twenty-five years working in the aircraft industry, the last ten in aircraft design, I wanted a job that would take all of that knowledge and skill and combine it into one role. I'd worked on various parts of aircraft wings and now I wanted to be the Lead Weights Engineer of the whole wing. As well as that I wanted to work on business aircraft and lastly I wanted to work abroad. I thought that that was a big list and sent it off into the Universe to see what happened.

Six weeks later, I'd more or less forgotten about what I wanted when I got an email, "How would you like to work in Toronto, Canada?"

In exchange for my updated CV they gave me the hourly rate, $70. I had to Google what that was in pounds, but it was more than I expected. In answer to my question, what was the project, I was informed that it was a new business jet.

Six weeks later my daughter and I arrived in Toronto, and three months later I was put in charge of the Wing Weights design. The job was exactly what I had asked for, with a pay that far exceeded my expectations.

A New Home

By Jane Mate

When I got divorced I lived in Malvern in Worcestershire I was renting a home that as a single Mom of three children was very expensive.

I was wanting to buy my own home and my best friend who lived in Wales said that houses there were are better value. I was unsure about uprooting us all to Wales 150 miles away.

However, the homes were very expensive in Worcestershire, so I started internet searches to find me and my family our new home!

I didn't have a big mortgage offer, but I am surprised I even got one. Internet searching in South Wales near my friend was fun. I found one online and booked a viewing on a Saturday at 6 pm.

My friend came with me but I was gutted it wasn't what I expected, the area was not suitable.

Following my viewing I had a coffee before starting the long journey home. There was an estate agents office near the café and this old guy, bless him, was still in the office.

As I was peering in the window at about 7.30pm the guy came out the shop and asked if he could help me. I told him my budget, and that I needed 3 bedrooms, I went on to say that I'd love the stone-fronted properties and a nice view would be good.

Waiting for him to laugh at my request he said, "I do have that house and it's empty and you can view it now if you wish to save you another journey". I said, "Yes please". I called my friend who thought I was joking but came to view the house.

Needless to say I put an offer in there and then and 3 weeks later moved in. This house ticked everything I asked for. Okay it needed a lot of work as it's an old house - the previous owner was over 100 years old and had lived there most of her life so it was quite dated.

The house had a nice atmosphere and I later found out the previous owner's husband was a miner all his life and it's an old miner cottage. It had exactly the stone front I wanted and the most lovely view to see every day opposite the farm.

My wonderful neighbour welcomed us and she had two children the same ages as my two. She is the same age as me and is also divorced and we are now lovely friends.

Move To New Country

By Purvi

I have been a very strong manifester throughout my life. Though some things have taken a bit longer than usual, I knew the Universe was clearing its way for me to have those things my life.

My biggest manifestation to date has been my move to the UK. I have always been a nature lover and have always wanted to be around a lot of greenery and nature and I loved the weather (I come from a city which has a lot of high rise buildings and it gets to 50 degrees Centigrade from June to August).

Apart from the nature, I have always had a sense of belonging in this lush country so much so that I made sure my husband and I made a trip every year to the UK, sometimes even twice. We did this since 2010. And every single time I landed in the UK, I prayed to my Angels to bring me here permanently.

It was 2019 March, when my husband decided to quit the company he had worked for 16 years. I was a typical Dubai girl, having lived there for 40 years, and moving out from there to my birth country did not settle well within me.

I started calling upon my Angels and started working on various healing modalities to assist us with the best option. The day when my husband decided to hand his resignation in, his immediate boss offered him a position in the UK, in their head office. It was amazing and we moved to the UK in January 2020.

While it did take some time for my intention to manifest, I totally trusted the Universe that it was creating a path for me to have what I want in my life. I asked and left it to the Universe with the belief that it will manifest at the best possible time and also if it is for my highest good.

Time For A Watch

By Angela

Two years ago I manifested a watch for myself without even realising it at first.

My partner and I took one of our grandchildren into a shop in town so she could show us which ring she had decided upon for her birthday.

As we were leaving the shop, I glanced in a display cabinet and saw a watch that I admired. We continued on our way and I thought no more about the watch.

My partner and I went off on our holiday cruising the Mediterranean. Towards the end of the cruise an announcement was made advertising a sale of jewellery the following day.

Unusually, we decided to go along and soon spotted a watch in the sale which we both liked. Eventually between us we decided I should have the watch so we made the purchase.

A day or two later I had the realisation that the watch was identical to the one I had admired before our holiday. Upon returning home I went along to the shop and checked the cost of the watch. It was double the price we had paid on the ship. What an amazing thing to happen. Two years on I am still astounded at how this manifested.

More Inspiring Manifestations From Clients That Have Worked With Me:

Debt Free

By Julie

I have to share with you how you helped me manifest what feels like a whole new life. In a short amount of time everything changed. I went from feeling so stuck and trapped to manifesting the most perfect job, not only doing what I love but also feeling valued and appreciated. I know that this is down to working on my worthiness and clearing some blocks that had held me back. Each day I come home feeling fulfilled and I am excited to say I have met someone. I know it is early days but it feels really promising. Last week I paid off my final outstanding credit card bill and I feel in control of my finances and confident in my life. Thank you so much Amanda, it would have not been possible without you.

Healing Blocks & More

By Nancy Triplett

I met Amanda virtually in May or June of 2018. I have been a seeker of Spirit and Truth my entire life, yet, I was not able to manifest my desires nor did I feel connected to my own Spirit Team (Angels, Guides, and Guardians). I was already highly intuitive, but did not trust what I received so I "hid" my gifts. I knew I was supposed to help others by inspiring them to connect to their inner light which I could see so clearly, yet they could not see for themselves.

Amanda first of all taught me about having a Daily Practice of meditation, journaling, grounding and protecting, using gratitude and a variety of fun ways to keep myself focused. My life immediately began turning around and I started feeling very connected to my intuition. I was suddenly able to manifest unexpected money, a perfect for me job, gifts, and invitations to have fun. I wanted to know more!

I realized through Amanda's teachings I had some blocks that needed to be removed. My biggest one was around feelings of "not enough". I scheduled a blockage removing session with Amanda and it totally changed my life. She was able to very gently but effectively lead me back to my childhood and to my father. I had very bad feelings about him and I had known for many years I needed to forgive him and wanted to. Yet every time I would think of him, I would think "ugh" and I could literally feel myself pushing the feelings deeper and deeper until I thought I had gotten rid of them. Instead, I had just been causing the blockage to grow. With Amanda's help, we got to the root of it all, and just like that, I began to forgive and heal. It wasn't just my father that played out in all of it either. My ex-husband had also been part of my need to forgive, and that process started also.

A few weeks after my session with Amanda, I was having a drive in our beautiful mountains. I was receiving information from my Spirit Team and suddenly was able to see my father, my ex-husband

and several others as I would anyone in my life....
just a child of God doing their best to work through
their life challenges! What a great day for freedom!

I have to say, the past two years have finally
brought together all the years prior that I have been
working on my spiritual evolution. I am so grateful
to have met Amanda and all the help she has given
me. I joined her High Vibe community "Abundance
Club" and the community and support I receive is
worth every penny spent!

Believing In Yourself

By Kim Snow

Amanda and the use of her many strategies have
changed my life for the better! I now know I can
ask my Angels for anything. I have manifested many
things big and small: a new car, money, and most
importantly inner peace!

The one thing that continues to blow my mind is
a 7.5 ft. mermaid sculpture. I have never sculpted
before and I have a passion for the environment and
plastic pollution. I wanted to make a difference. I
followed my guidance and trusted my Angels every
step of the way.

Every time I got stuck I asked my Angels for
support and whatever I needed appeared. When I
look at her now, I cannot believe I made her.

I know her purpose is to draw attention to single use plastic in the ocean and I have my Angels to thank for her. She has also inspired me to make other pieces and now I will supplement my income with my artwork!

Whatever you dream of can be yours. Keep to a practice, believe that all is possible, and trust that it is coming to you! It truly works!

Happy Manifesting!

Booked Up 2 Weeks In Advanced

By Elizabeth Walton

After being in your group Abundance Manifesting (Free group) for a while and taking the Abundance Reset Challenge my life has changed immensely!

There are so many manifesting stories I could tell you about.

I was manifesting that my business would pick up and that I would be successful. I posted this in the group.

In one of Amanda's video she spoke of be, do, have.

What would you have to do if you already had what you wanted? It made complete sense and I knew what I had to do. I greatly decreased what I was giving away for free and told everyone I had to clear my calendar for paying clients and to help balance things out for my family.

Incredibly it worked. I am now booking 2 weeks in advance for my business! Manifesting works! Thank you Amanda Tooke! You are an Angel!

There are many other things to say but I am now a true believer in manifesting!! Not only that but during the challenge I kept picturing Amanda's book and cards in my Sacred Space and low and behold if I won them! I absolutely love both and use the cards daily!

Thank you from the bottom of my heart Amanda. Life is so much calmer and peaceful since becoming a member of your group!

Useful Links

Here you will find all the links and references I have mentioned through the book.

FREE RESOURCES
Come and connect with me in my free community which is always open over on Facebook.

www.facebook.com/groups/AbunMan

If you head on over to:
www.theangelmystic.co.uk/mmbook/
you will find free manifesting resources to help you on your journey such as meditations and other tools.

MONTHLY MEMBERSHIP SITE
Abundance Club

If you would like to take your manifesting one step further you may be interested in joining my private manifesting club – Abundance Club.

I only open the doors a few times a year to new members, but please check it out here if we are accepting new members **www.theangelmystic.co.uk/mmbook/**

If not you will be able to add your name to the list to be notified next time the doors open.

SHOP

Over on my website...

www.theangelmystic.co.uk/mmbook

you will find my books and other products.

Do I have an Angel?

A down to earth guide about "The Upstairs"
Everything you need to know about your Angels.
(You can also find this on Amazon
as paperback or Kindle).

Manifesting Journal

If you have ever bought a journal or indeed a notepad with the intention of using it as a journal but then had no idea what to do then this is for you.

Within this special journal that I have created, you will find help in 4 ways:

1. Help hold yourself accountable to your daily practice.

2. Keep you on track with your manifesting.

3. Help with your communication with your Angel.

4. Support your journaling and healing journey.

It is ideal to use with **The Angel Mystic's Manifesting Manual** or **Abundance Club**.

The Basics – MP3

Learn to fully ground and protect yourself with simple exercises, it is like a spiritual tool box so you can pick and choose from various exercises to see what works best for you.

Angel Meditations – MP3

This is the perfect meditation selection to start off with when you are learning to connect with your Angel. It is 3 meditations plus grounding and protection exercises that will enable you to connect with your Angel, heal with the Archangels and start to manifest the life you want.

Rainbow Healing – MP3

These are powerful healing meditations, as forgiveness and unconditional love is something the Angels talk about all the time; it sets you free from your past.

These three meditations are to rebalance your Chakras, work on Forgiveness and Unconditional Love,

so that you can address the blocks and issues that are holding you back and move forward positively with your Angel's help.

Angel Cards
My awesome unique Angel Cards

My Angel Cards are incredibly accurate and easy to use.
The simple design delivers
a powerful clear message.
You will find it fun pulling a
card a day to give you your
daily guidance or you can
do a full reading with them.
They are a great way of
getting messages yourself

and deepening your relationship with your Angel. They are easy to shuffle and fit perfectly even in the smallest of hands, so children love them too.

There is no right and no wrong with these cards, they are all about using your intuition, but as a guide each set comes with a full instruction leaflet and a meaning leaflet for each card.

Enchanted Life
My best selling Angel Programme

Learn to connect with your Guardian Angel so you can feel more support in day to day life. You have an Angel ready, willing and able to help you with everything; emotional and practical help. This programme will help you access this and build an ever growing relationship with your Angels.

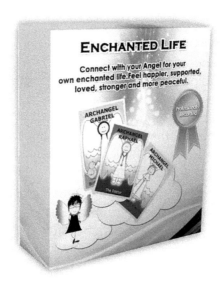

Create Abundance in 14 Days

Each day for 14 days I will send you via email a new exercise to expand your wealth consciousness and help heal your money story, so you can attract more abundance into your life.

Learn to play with the Universe with this fantastic programme, as each day you get to try a new manifesting exercise.

Ingram Content Group UK Ltd.
Milton Keynes UK
UKHW020922260423
420810UK00015B/626

9 781913 898052